ABOUT

, MARTIN.

, ABOUT

REAM.'

SON
S SPEECH AT THE MARCH ON WASHINGTON

TIME

More than 200,000 people from all over the country traveled to the March on Washington, Aug. 28, 1963.

CALLED TO BE FREE

HOW THE CIVIL RIGHTS MOVEMENT CREATED A NEW NATION

FOREWORD BY
HENRY LOUIS GATES JR.

Visit time.com/onedream
to view TIME's multimedia
documentary project
featuring interviews with
men and women who took
part in the March
on Washington.

The Gathering *A multiracial crowd thronged the Mall to hear Martin Luther King Jr. and other speakers call for America to live up to the promises of the Declaration of Independence.*

Deliverance *Drinking from a segregated water fountain in North Carolina in 1950; Martin Luther King Jr. speaking to a crowd of 25,000 by the Lincoln Memorial at a 1957 prayer pilgrimage*

WE HAVE NOT COME THIS FAR ALONE

BY HENRY LOUIS GATES JR.

As I sat on the steps of the Lincoln Memorial last August listening to my hero, Congressman John Lewis, commemorate the anniversary of the March on Washington, I found myself reflecting on the long sweep of historical events that made this particular historical event possible. It suddenly dawned on me that the long glassy pool at my back was designed to encourage this kind of reflection, functioning as a sort of double entendre, reflection both literal and figurative. I was struck by the diversity of the faces that surrounded me, attesting to the fact that "The March," as we all called it, had been 50 years ago, and continued today to be appreciated as a truly American story by a rising generation drinking in the hard-earned wisdom of the original march's last surviving speaker, a survivor with the scars of the movement's climactic struggles still visible in his face. As I listened, I thought not only about the transformative events of 50 years ago, a time when I was not quite 13, but of the entire 500-year sweep of history that has defined the African American experience. And what an epic history it is: one that has crossed many rivers, from the first free black man, a conquistador, to arrive in Florida in 1513, through the long-dark centuries of enslavement; from a bloody civil war to the jubilee of emancipation; from the birth of Jim Crow segregation in the 1890s to the deliverance of the civil rights movement; from the most insidious Supreme Court decisions throughout the 19th century, to the swearing in, by the Chief Justice of the Supreme Court, of our first black

Historic Climax *On the march from Selma to Montgomery fighting for the vote; President Obama sitting on the famed bus Rosa Parks rode, now at the Henry Ford Museum in Dearborn, Mich.*

president for the second time, and whose raised hand, beneath the Statue of Freedom, called to mind the irony of the fact that a slave's hands had cast that statue to crown the Capitol dome 150 years before.

Like Dr. King's last-minute decision to tell the marchers of 1963 about his "Dream" (thanks to the exhortations of Mahalia Jackson at his back), this longer journey of ours has been marked by countless improvisational acts born of a human desire to transcend all-too-human repressive practices. Out of the most painful circumstances, a people and a culture have revolutionized the nation by narrowing the yawning gap between its revolutionary ideals and its laws. As Carter G. Woodson, the founder of Black History Week, told us almost a century ago, "the accounts of the successful strivings of Negroes for enlightenment under most adverse circumstances read like beautiful romances of a people in an heroic age." Aspiration, agitation, activism: these have always been the hallmarks of our "romance," unexpectedly unfolding across time with all of the drama that underscores the most classic of sagas.

What else could have propelled Juan Garrido, the conquistador, to become the first black explorer to cross the Atlantic Ocean looking for the Fountain of Youth in 1513, as an equal along with Ponce de Leon? What else can explain why generations of slaves, possessed with nothing more than the most fundamental human desires—the right to live free and earn a living freely—risked all to escape to all-black settlements, as early as the late 17th century in a remote outpost of northern Florida, and eventually as far north as Canada? Or why they revolted against their masters—sometimes violently, more often with subtlety—and their descendants, once free, migrated in great waves up and out of the South seeking jobs?

"Agitate! Agitate! Agitate!"—that's what the former slave and black abolitionist Frederick Douglass had urged those coming up behind him to do, and from the beginning of their days of despair in this country, they did just that, agitating for their rights by launching newspapers, penning slave narratives, building churches and schools, and fighting for their country in every one of its wars even when that country was unwilling to recognize them as citizens, or even as men. Of course, all three of these elements animated the planners of that game-changing march in August 1963, galvanizing men and women, young and old, black and white, to teach the world the power of nonviolent protest by demanding justice inside court and legislative chambers while risking the greatest of injustices to themselves and their families in the streets—from tree limbs, from lampposts, in church basements and atop bridges and hotel balconies.

No one understood this history better than the Rev. Dr. Martin Luther King Jr. himself. In the metaphor he shared at the Lincoln Memorial—of the check returned and marked "insufficient funds" a century after President Lincoln signed the Emancipation Proclamation—he was reminding us all that as much as the African American people needed the nation to safeguard their rights, for centuries the nation had benefited from their uncompensated toil. And the country profited, I might add, from the genius of their creations fusing European cultural forms with African cultural forms to create a truly American culture, exportable to the world—from the spirituals to the blues, from ragtime to jazz, from rhythm and blues and soul to hip-hop.

Each of these reflections, and more, were dancing within me while I listened to John Lewis speak at the Lincoln Memorial last August. I remembered what it was like to watch the original on (black-and-white) TV with my parents in our living room back in Piedmont, W. Va., and was delighted to be standing there in person 50 years on with my friend Glenn Hutchins and his mother, Marguerite, who had attended the first March on Washington and asked her son to bring her to the commemoration, in a wheelchair, as her 93rd birthday present. I was proud, exceedingly proud, of all that we have achieved since 1963 through advances in higher education enabled by affirmative action, through the flowering of our black professional ranks and the quadrupling of the black upper middle class since King's death in 1968. At the same time, I, like many around me, was ever more conscious of the "unfinished work" of our story, to borrow from President Lincoln, much of which can be summed up in a single word—inequality—which has persisted, even worsened, in recent years. The explosive growth in the black upper middle class has been offset by the large percentage of the poorest among us—the chronically poor—still trapped in child poverty, being "mis-educated," as Woodson famously put it, in underfunded, dangerous, crumbling schools, disproportionately represented in overcrowded prisons and blighted inner cities—inequalities as close to King's heart as dismantling legal segregation was.

Fifty years after the march, 150 years after emancipation and 500 years since that first black conquistador set foot in the New World, there is no doubt that much work remains to be done if we are to fulfill the promise of America for all of its citizens, including the sons and daughters of the slaves. As I sat next to Glenn and Miss Marguerite, one of the few living veterans of both marches, it occurred to me that the speakers on the platform at the first march, and the hundreds of thousands of citizens surrounding the reflecting pool who composed their marching, triumphant audience, had been motivated by one common goal: the unshakable determination to teach America to dream again, to dream the dream of freedom upon which this great country of ours was founded, to make real its revolutionary ideals, so that they can be embraced by each of its citizens, regardless of race, gender, creed, national origin or class. After all, that was the promise that America held out to the world's nations, the fulfillment of the aspirations of millennia of the world's great civilizations. And so I close with two of my favorite lines from the black tradition: "We've come this far by faith" and "We have not come this far alone." May these words continue to guide us for the next 50—indeed, the next 500—years.

Henry Louis Gates Jr. is the director of the Hutchins Center for African and African American Research at Harvard University, editor in chief of TheRoot.com and host of the PBS series The African Americans: Many Rivers to Cross.

A DREAM FORETOLD

LONG BEFORE MARTIN LUTHER KING'S PIVOTAL
SPEECH, AFRICAN AMERICANS HAD BEEN STEADILY
BUILDING THE FOUNDATION OF EQUALITY FOR ALL

BY PATRIK HENRY BASS

"**FIVE SCORE YEARS** ago, a great American, in whose symbolic shadow we stand today, signed the Emancipation Proclamation," said Martin Luther King Jr. on August 28, 1963, seconds into "I Have a Dream," his masterpiece of rhetoric and oratory. Before a rapt sea of more than 250,000 people, he continued: "This momentous decree came as a great beacon light of hope to millions of Negro slaves who had been seared in the flames of withering injustice. It came as a joyous daybreak to end the long night of their captivity." Under one sun and a stoic Abraham Lincoln's watchful eye, King raised the spirits and hopes of the descendants of slaves and their owners; of abolitionists, black and white, and their supporters and detractors. Then his next sentence tempered the message: "But 100 years later, the Negro still is not free."

Like many who have been otherwise hypnotized by the power and poetry of King's dream, I confess that, for many years—more than I care to admit—it was that last thought that lingered,

Freedom's Route
In May 1961, Freedom Riders wait at a Montgomery, Ala., bus station as they travel through the South to test a Supreme Court ruling that outlawed the segregation of public facilities used by interstate travelers.

undermining what came before. *The Negro still is not free.*

In just the preceding decade, this crowd had witnessed visible evidence of seminal American civil rights victories. Consider: in Brown v. Board of Education, the U.S. Supreme Court had declared in 1954 that segregated public schools were unconstitutional. Two years later, the court declared likewise about the segregated bus system in Montgomery, Ala., while the sit-ins in 1960 at a Woolworth's in Greensboro, N.C., brought about the integration of lunch counters across the South. This momentum was not an accident. From the founding of the country through the Civil War and two world wars, there had been breakthroughs and many more setbacks on the long road to equality for all, and on this day in 1963, in a few short words, King brought all to a national crossroads.

It was, of course, with good reason that the March on Washington ended up where it did. Lincoln was the first of our presidents who set out to reconcile the one woeful contradiction of the Declaration of Independence. Before him, the inalienable rights of life, liberty and the pursuit of happiness were not afforded those black patriots who fought in the Revolutionary War or their brothers and sisters whose labor was so vital to America's ascendence. What was both guide map and safety net for those who had in common maleness and whiteness was neither for the vast enslaved population that was scattered throughout the South and parts of the Northeast. *Life?* Their bodies belonged to their owners and sometimes were worth less than a head of cattle. *Liberty?* They could go only where they were told. *Pursuit of happiness?* Most were forbidden even to read and write; in some states, doing so was a serious offense.

But the ideals of the Declaration of Independence were lost on the more fortunate among them too. By the turn of the 19th century, there was a sizable community of "free people of color" in the U.S. A few were born free, but others had left enslavement, many wearing their finest outfits, only to end up in free states, shirtless, shoeless, hopeless. Though they may have been called freemen and freewomen, in every other regard they had little or no protections under the law. They were banned from white-owned hotels, restaurants and theaters. Most churches charged them to attend and sat them apart from white congregants. Only a handful of free blacks could vote, and in many regions they were not allowed to own property. All the while, Blackbirders posed a constant threat. Those kidnappers snatched freemen and escaped slaves off the streets and from their homes and sent them south to a life of hard labor, privation and punishment.

In the mid-1820s, M. Boston Crummell invited a group of free blacks, including John Russwurm and Samuel Cornish, to his well-appointed home in New York City. Born a slave, Crummell had made himself into a successful oyster vendor. (His son, Alexander, grew up to become a prominent minister and African nationalist.) Crummell and his colleagues valiantly mounted a multitiered strategy to address the country's inequities. The first was to create a national vehicle to spread the word about their cause for full freedom. In 1827, they launched *Freedom's Journal*, America's first black newspaper. That paper was short-lived, but it spawned many subsequent black newspapers and a growing wave of support for the cause. In print, public halls and private parlors, the battle was being joined. Ministers and educators; porters, barbers, bootblacks and stevedores, hairdressers, janitors, chimney sweeps, furniture makers, butchers, tailors, clerks, shoemakers, domestics, seafarers, nursemaids, tailors, carpenters and coachmen. Together they quietly (and sometimes loudly) gathered to advocate for equal status under the law.

Those who lived to witness that chilly first day of 1863 when Lincoln issued his historic proclamation may not have felt the earth's plates move beneath them, but there could be no denying that something fundamental had shifted. If expectation soon gave way to disappointment, it

Frederick Douglass
Douglass fled slavery in 1838, and through his speeches and writings became one of the main voices of abolitionism. He assisted fugitives along the Underground Railroad, conferred with Abraham Lincoln, and after the Civil War carried on the fight not only for the rights of blacks but also women.

Harriet Beecher Stowe
Her bestselling book *Uncle Tom's Cabin* forced the brutality of slavery into the consciousness of America and galvanized those opposed to the "curious institution." Upon meeting Stowe, President Lincoln noted, "So you're the little woman who wrote the book that started this great war."

Abraham Lincoln
On January 1, 1863, the president issued the Emancipation Proclamation, an executive order that made the Confederacy's slaves "forever free." More important, it elevated the destruction of slavery to a central purpose of the Civil War, which until then was focused on the preservation of the Union.

was not born of disillusionment. As historian John Hope Franklin has noted, "Lincoln went as far as he felt the law permitted him to go." And soon after, abolitionist Henry Ward Beecher stood before a packed congregation in Brooklyn's Plymouth Church and said, "The Proclamation may not free a single slave, but it gives liberty a moral recognition." Indeed, it was the 13th Amendment, ratified nearly three years later, that ultimately abolished enslavement, and even it could not quickly and easily erase every remnant of the offending system. And so those 100 years that Dr. King spoke of continued to be filled with violence and valor.

In 1864, freed blacks gathered in Syracuse, N.Y., for the first of what were to become annual conventions. Combining the full might of clergy, congregants, activists and educators, these meetings were essential in unifying a rising African American professional and political class. Several among them served in the 41st through 45th Congresses of the U.S.: Senator Hiram R. Revels of Mississippi and representatives Benjamin S. Turner, Josiah T. Walls, Joseph H. Rainey, Robert Brown Elliott, Robert C. De Large and Jefferson F. Long. By 1891, more than 2,390 African Americans were working for the federal government in Washington, D.C., earning salaries that totaled $1,370,000.

But the rest of American society and the country's courts were not nearly as receptive. On June 7, 1892, Homer Plessy, a "creole of color," was jailed for sitting in the whites-only section of an East Louisiana Railroad train. Plessy, who was in fact one-eighth black, was protesting the Separate Car Act, a state law that segregated common transportation carriers. Four years later, Plessy v. Ferguson made its way to the Supreme Court, where Justice Henry Brown, speaking for a seven-man majority, upheld the law. "A statute which implies merely a legal distinction between the white and colored races ... has no tendency to destroy the legal equality of the two races," he wrote. The Fourteenth Amendment, he continued, "could not have been intended to abolish distinctions based upon color, or to enforce social, as distinguished from political, equality, or a commingling of the two races upon terms unsatisfactory to either." (John Harlan, the sole dissenting Justice, wrote in response, "Our Constitution is color-blind, and neither knows nor tolerates classes among citizens. In respect of civil rights, all citizens are equal before the law.")

The Plessy decision confirmed for America's black men and women the need to forcefully press for their civil rights. A decade later, as the 20th century dawned, sociologist W.E.B. Du Bois, *Boston Guardian* editor William Monroe Trotter, and two dozen other men convened at Niagara Falls—on the Canadian side because no hotel in nearby Buffalo, N.Y., would accommodate them—and again a year later in Harpers Ferry, West Virginia. Du Bois's group, which by his own description was dedicated to "organized, determined and aggressive action," chose that rendezvous to commemorate John Brown, the controversial abolitionist who tried to spark a slave rebellion by sacking the federal armory there in 1859. But it was a 1909 meeting in New York City that cast the longest shadow, resulting in the founding of the National Association for the Advancement of Colored People. The NAACP methodically set out to end segregation and discrimination in employment, voting, housing, education and transportation, and to finally persuade national leaders of the evils of condoned practices like lynching. In 1940, the organization launched its Legal Defense and Educational Fund under the direction of attorney Thurgood Marshall, to fight public school segregation.

The NAACP wasn't fighting alone. In 1941, as World War II roiled, influential Brotherhood of Sleeping Car Porters union leader A. Philip Randolph, along with activist Bayard Rustin and labor-relations leader Anna Arnold Hedgeman, headed up a challenge against the discriminatory hiring practices of defense plants. Using the methods Crummell devised a century before, Randolph drummed up interest among the black press, ministers, educators, politicians and Walter White, the executive director of the NAACP, for a March on Washington Movement. It never came to pass, but tens of thousands of people had been galvanized, and First Lady Eleanor Roosevelt, who was an NAACP national board member, had brokered a conversation between Randolph and her husband. At the White House, even as President Roosevelt recognized the importance of the cause, he advised caution, worried about the potential for violence in the nation's capital and about how America's enemies in the impending war might exploit it. Yet Randolph pressed forward, and on June 25, 1941, FDR signed Executive Order 8802 banning racial discrimination in America's defense industry.

The order was an important step toward what became known as the Era of Rising Expectations for African Americans. The postwar years transformed this nation, exerting a profound influence on the everyday lives and expectations of its citizens. Returning GIs comfortably settled into immaculate new homes and traveled to work in glistening Pontiacs and Buicks. Wives joined the PTA and shared chicken divan recipes with neighbors at Tupperware parties. From the New Look to the New Frontier, never had the country experienced so many social, cultural and political milestones or achieved such remarkable economic progress. No segment of society was left untouched by the boom.

And that included, for the first time, the black community. African American home ownership soared and incomes leapt. Literacy was at an all-time high, with 24 of every 25 blacks between the age of 14 and 24 able to read and write. Birth rates swelled as infant mortality fell. Over 75%

P.B.S. Pinchback
The Louisiana politician was the nation's first black governor. He later headed to the U.S. House and Senate, though opponents prevented him from taking up the position. Pinchback's career was emblematic of the difficulties blacks faced in trying to gain a foothold on political power.

Booker T. Washington
Born a Virginia slave, the leader and educator founded the Tuskegee Normal and Industrial Institute to educate blacks. Washington insisted that to get ahead, blacks needed to focus on economic progress while temporarily abandoning their efforts toward political advancement.

Ida B. Wells-Barnett
Following the lynching of a friend, the journalist crusaded against the practice, which was used to terrorize black citizens and businesses. Her influential pamphlet *Southern Horrors* called on blacks to use rifles and any other means at their disposal to protect their families.

of black households were led by a husband and wife. Security and stability were imaginable; professional and personal achievement plausible. A groundswell of confidence engulfed African American communities everywhere. This was the moment, and those who had been pushing all along for equal rights saw that there could be no turning back.

Marshall and his colleagues at the NAACP were in the midst of their 20-year campaign to chip away at segregated schools, an effort that culminated in the early 1950s when Marshall argued in Brown v. Board of Education that African American students were being denied equal protection under the law by being kept out of all-white public schools, and in 1954 the Supreme Court agreed. In a unanimous ruling, the court found that the "separate but equal" doctrine once codified by Plessy was unconstitutional. The following year, a seamstress and NAACP member named Rosa Louise McCauley Parks was arrested in Montgomery, Ala., for violating a law that held that a black person must surrender a bus seat to a white person if asked before moving to the "colored" section in the back. From a small Southern city, this tiny, elegant woman caught the attention of the nation, the world, and one new minister in town. Not long after Martin Luther King Jr. helped to organize a local bus boycott to highlight the wrongness of the rule, the Supreme Court agreed. Parks's refusal to be treated differently ushered in the modern civil rights movement. The Negro was still not free, but that wouldn't be the case for much longer.

Patrik Henry Bass is editorial projects director at Essence *and the author of* Like a Mighty Stream: The March on Washington, August 28, 1963.

Victory *Rosa Parks (in glasses and hat) rides on a newly integrated city bus following the successful Montgomery bus boycott of 1955.*

LIBERATING IMAGES

PHOTOS FROM THE 'JIM CROW' SOUTH
STARTLED AMERICA AND SPURRED
WASHINGTON INTO ACTION

BY BEN COSGROVE

Undaunted *White Arkansans jeer 15-year-old Elizabeth Eckford, one of the famous "Little Rock Nine," during the September 1957 integration of Little Rock Central High School.*

TODAY, WHEN SEEMINGLY every event, no matter how insignificant or

momentous, is captured on some sort of video device, shared and often forgotten within minutes, it's difficult to imagine a time when the still image—the photograph—served as the lens through which people experienced the news. For the civil rights movement, photos helped change the course of history. When Americans outside the Deep South saw protestors being attacked by the authorities, the resulting outrage pushed presidents into action and Congress toward changing the laws. At the forefront of documenting segregation was *Life*, TIME's sister publication. While its coverage of the Jim Crow South strove to be fair, *Life*'s pictures were often, in effect, indictments of a great nation's most bitter failing. In the 1950s, the self-evident truth that all men and women are created equal was difficult to discern through images of tear gas, the smoke of burning churches and schoolhouses, and the spray of fire hoses turned on nonviolent protestors. In such an environment, *Life*'s photographs, some of them shown here, did not simply report the news; they bore witness to outrage and defiance on both sides of the desegregation divide.

Traveling with the photojournalists were reporters, who got the story of their lives. "The Northern press would parachute in reporters when news broke," remembers Richard Stolley, a former *Life* editor who spent four years in the South as a correspondent for the magazine in

Seat of Power *Graduate student Virginius B. Thornton and other activists participate in a sit-down strike at a whites-only lunch counter in Petersburg, Va., in 1960.*

the mid 1950s, "and when the story was over they'd leave. But TIME, *Life, Newsweek* and a few others had staff there, and it made all the difference. White Southerners were hesitant to talk with a 'Yankee' publication, but when they asked where we were from and we could answer, honestly, 'We live in Atlanta,' you could see their attitude change. They might not like us, but they'd speak with us. "

Life's rival publication, *Look,* had its own powerful stories. In the summer of 1955, two men, both of them white, abducted a 14-year-old African American boy named Emmett Till from his great-uncle's house in Money, Miss. Roy Bryant and J.W. Milam beat Till almost to death, gouged out one of his eyes, shot him in the head and dumped his body in the Tallahatchie River. Their motive: Till, visiting from his native Chicago, had reportedly flirted with (or, according to some accounts, spoken "disrespectfully") to Bryant's wife a few days before. When an all-white, all-male jury acquitted Bryant and Milam of kidnapping and murder, the verdict shocked observers across the U.S. And when, months later, the men admitted to *Look* that they had, in fact, mutilated and murdered Till, the outcry was so intense—and the reaction of Till's family so dignified—that it lit a spark that helped ignite the modern civil rights movement.

At LIFE.com, find the stories behind many of the greatest civil rights photographs ever made.

Immovable *Pummeled by water from a fire hose trained on them by city firefighters, civil rights demonstrators reel against a storefront in Birmingham, Ala., in the spring of 1963.*

THE MAN AND THE MARCH THAT CHANGED AMERICA

The Dream Delivered
Martin Luther King Jr., photographed moments after giving his speech at the March on Washington, Aug. 28, 1963.

We Shall Overcome *John F. Kennedy worried that a civil rights demonstration in the nation's capital would erupt into violence. But peace and solidarity won the day, with movement leaders, including Andrew Young, second row center, and Julian Bond, second row far right, mixing with the crowd.*

Strength in Numbers *The march drew 250,000 to the National Mall. It was the largest demonstration to date in American history.*

A King Among Men
Leaving the podium, King is congratulated after his speech. He improvised the dream passage at the urging of Mahalia Jackson (left, in hat).

BY JON MEACHAM

IT WAS NOT GOING WELL,

or at least not as well as Martin Luther King Jr. had hoped. The afternoon had been long: the crowds massed before the Lincoln Memorial were ready for some rhetorical adrenaline, some true poetry. King's task now was to lift his speech from the ordinary to the historic, from the mundane to the sacred. He was enjoying the greatest audience of his life. Yet with the television networks broadcasting live and President Kennedy watching from the White

His Grandest Pulpit *Speech in hand, King acknowledges the crowd that came to hear him and others speak for equality, justice and jobs.*

House, King was struggling with a text that had been drafted by too many hands late the previous night at the Willard Hotel. One sentence he was about to deliver was particularly awkward: "And so today, let us go back to our communities as members of the international association for the advancement of creative dissatisfaction." King was on the verge of letting the hour pass him by.

Then, as on Easter morning at the tomb of the crucified Jesus, there was the sound of a woman's voice. King had already begun to extemporize when Mahalia Jackson spoke up. "Tell 'em about the dream, Martin," said Jackson, who was standing nearby. King left his text altogether at this point—a departure that put him on a path to speaking words of American scripture, words as essential to the nation's destiny in their way as those of Abraham Lincoln, before whose memorial King stood, and those of Thomas Jefferson, whose monument lay to the preacher's right, toward the Potomac. The moments of ensuing oratory lifted King above the tumult of history and made him a figure of history, a "new founding father," in the apt phrase of the historian Taylor Branch.

"I say to you today, my friends ... even though we face the difficulties of today and tomorrow, I still have a dream," King said. "It is a dream deeply rooted in the American Dream"—a dream that had been best captured in the promise of words written in a distant summer in Philadelphia by Jefferson. "I have a dream," King continued, "that one day this nation will rise up, live out the true meaning of its creed: 'We hold these truths to be self-evident, that all men are created equal.' "

Drawing on the Bible and "My Country, 'Tis of Thee," on the Emancipation Proclamation and the Constitution, King, like Jefferson and Lincoln before him, projected an ideal vision of an exceptional nation. In King's imagined country, hope triumphed over the fear that life is only about what Thomas Hobbes called the "war of all against all" rather than equal justice for all. In doing so, King defined the best of the nation as surely as Jefferson did in Philadelphia in 1776 or Lincoln did at Gettysburg in 1863.

"I have a dream that one day on the red hills of Georgia, sons of former slaves and the sons of former slave owners will be able to sit down together at the table of brotherhood.

I have a dream that one day even the state of Mississippi, a state sweltering with the heat of injustice, sweltering with the heat of oppression, will be transformed into an oasis of freedom and justice.

I have a dream that my four little children will one day live in a nation where they will not be judged by the color of their skin but by the content of their character...

I have a dream today."

Fifty years on, no matter where one stands on the political spectrum, it's all too easy to be glib about the meaning of the March on Washington and the movement's victories: the 1964 Civil Rights Act and the 1965 Voting Rights Act. For some conservatives, the civil rights movement belongs to a kind of antiquity. In striking down a key section of the 1965 voting-rights legislation (a bill consistently renewed by Congress, including as recently as 2006 for an additional 25 years), Chief Justice John Roberts wrote that "our country has changed" and that the discriminatory world where African Americans were blocked from the ballot box no longer exists. On the other extreme, there are liberals who believe that racial progress has been so glacial—never mind gradual—that the shooting of a young man like Trayvon Martin (and the subsequent acquittal of his killer) is all too often the rule rather than the exception in America.

The prevailing reality—and a crucial legacy—of King's speech to the nation 50 years ago

We Cannot Walk Alone *King and his circle join the 250,000 protesters marching to the Lincoln Memorial.*

may have been best captured last summer, in the wake of the Martin verdict, when a particular African American calmly enumerated the daily acts of racism that still shape our national life. "There are very few African American men in this country who haven't had the experience of being followed when they were shopping in a department store. That includes me. And there are very few African American men who haven't had the experience of walking across the street and hearing the locks click on the doors of cars. That happens to me, at least before I was a senator. There are very few African Americans who haven't had the experience of getting on an elevator and a woman clutching her purse nervously and holding her breath until she had a chance to get off. That happens often."

A gloomy report. And yet, and yet: the black man making these observations in the James Brady Briefing Room of the White House was the 44th president of the United States, Barack Obama, who was a toddler when Martin Luther King Jr. stepped up to the podium at the march in 1963.

The most obvious observation about life since August 1963 is also the most accurate: we have traveled far, but not far enough. Revisiting King's speech, the religiously infused culture from which it sprang, and the political moment in which he delivered it suggests that King, for one, wouldn't be especially surprised by the ambivalent state of affairs in the America of today. Like our more familiar founders (Washington, Adams, Hamilton, Jefferson), he was a practical idealist, a man who could articulate an ideal but knew that human progress, while

High Note *Mahalia Jackson sings "I Been 'Buked and I Been Scorned" from the podium.*

sometimes intoxicatingly rapid, tends to be a provisional enterprise. The march, he said that day in Washington, was not an end; it was but a beginning. We live in a world King helped create. We do not yet live in the world he helped all of us dream of.

It is tempting to romanticize the words he spoke before the Lincoln Memorial. To do so, however, cheapens the courage of the known and the unknown nonviolent soldiers of freedom who faced—and often paid—the ultimate price for daring America to live up to the implications of the Declaration of Independence and become a country in which liberty was innate and universal, not particular to station, creed or color. The true honor we can give to King and his comrades is not to render them as fantastical figures in a Manichaean struggle but to see them as human beings who summoned the will to make the rest of us be the people we ought to be.

The death of Jim Crow is an epic story, but it is no fairy tale, for the half-century since the March on Washington has surely taught us that while African Americans are largely living happier lives, no one can sensibly say that everyone is living happily ever after. The dream of which King spoke was less a dream to bring about on this side of paradise than a prophetic vision to be approximated, for King's understanding of equality and brotherhood was much likelier to be realized in the kingdom of God than in any mortal realm. In Washington to demand legislative action, King spoke as a minister of the Lord, invoking the meaning of the Sermon on the Mount in a city more often interested in the mechanics of the Senate.

However unreachable his dream seems to be on this side of paradise, though, we must try. Like the promises of the Declaration of Independence or the Gettysburg Address or FDR's First Inaugural ("The only thing we have to fear is fear itself"), the promises of King's "I Have a Dream" sermon can be kept only if the nation is mindful of what Lincoln called "the better angels of our nature." In his words to the March on Washington, Martin Luther King Jr. gave us a standard against which we could forever measure ourselves and our nation. So long as his dream proves elusive, then our union remains imperfect.

A WEDNESDAY IN WASHINGTON

White Washington had expected mayhem. Few bureaucrats or lawyers who worked downtown in the capital showed up for work on Wednesday, Aug. 28, 1963. That many blacks? In one place? Who knew what might happen? Even the ordinarily liberal *New York Times* was wary. "There was great fear there would be rioting," recalled the *Times*'s Russell Baker, who was assigned a front-page feature on the march, "so the *Times* chartered a chopper." Boarding the helicopter early in the day, Baker grew so bored by the peaceable spectacle that he asked the pilot to fly over his house so he could check on the condition of his roof. "Finally," said Baker, "I had him land at National Airport and went to the Lincoln Memorial."

It was, it turned out, not only orderly but also integrated. Baker wrote of Bob Dylan, Charlton Heston and Marlon Brando; the paper took note of the series of speeches and songs, including Jackson's "I Been 'Buked and I Been Scorned," a spiritual delivered with such power that Baker reported that Jackson's voice seemed to echo off the far-off Capitol. Speaker after speaker—the young John Lewis, the aged A. Philip Randolph—made the case for racial justice. "For many, the day seemed an adventure, a long outing in the late summer sun—part liberation from home, part Sunday School picnic, part political convention, and part fish-fry," James Reston wrote in his piece for the *Times* the next day.

Watching King's speech in the White House, Kennedy listened with appreciation, then readied for a meeting with the march's leadership to discuss the practical steps ahead to push legislation through a Congress still dominated by white-segregationist Democrats. The ensuing session did not produce much in the way of progress. Kennedy feared moving too quickly, and as they had said again and again all afternoon, the civil rights delegation from the Mall believed the time for action was at hand. Yet King, who craved forward motion, had spoken of delay and of dreams deferred. The pilgrimage would be long, he had told his listeners, and the pilgrims had to maintain the moral high ground they had so effectively claimed through nonviolence. "And that is something that I must say to my people who stand on the worn threshold which leads into the palace of justice," King had told the crowd. "In the process of gaining our rightful place, we must not be guilty of wrongful deeds ... We must forever conduct our struggle on the high plane of dignity and discipline." If the politicians were too slow, well, that meant there had to be yet more dignity and yet more discipline.

The *Times*'s Reston, a reliable barometer of Establishment opinion, however, believed the day had in fact accomplished something, even if JFK was less than enthusiastic late that afternoon. "The demonstration impressed political Washington because it combined a number of things no politician can ignore," wrote Reston. "It had the force of numbers. It had the melodies of both the church and the theater. And it was able to invoke the principles of the founding fathers to rebuke the inequalities and hypocrisies of modern American life."

FREEDOM—SORT OF—AT LAST

Kennedy had not met with King and his comrades alone on the afternoon of Aug. 28. In the president's party was his generally unhappy vice president, Lyndon Johnson.

It's a tragic irony of American history that a people enslaved by white men finally became equal before the law not because of the nonviolent courage of millions of people of color but because of the murder of a single white man. The horror of the bombing of the 16th Street Baptist Church in Birmingham, Ala., on Sept. 15, 1963—an attack executed by Klansmen that killed four young girls—loomed large in the national consciousness, particularly when the violence of the crime was contrasted with the nonviolence of the March on Washington. Yet there is no escaping the fact that the moral case King made before the nation in August 1963 was given legislative force only after the assassination of Kennedy in Dallas three months later elevated Johnson to the presidency. The passage of the landmark bills of 1964 and 1965 was possible because LBJ was determined—but a determined realist. "Even if we pass this bill, the battle will not be over," he said after the Selma marches in March 1965 as he proposed voting-rights legislation.

It would, though, be a battle won. From the Brown school-desegregation decisions in 1954 and 1955 through the Great Society bills of the mid-1960s, Jim Crow was fatally wounded—so much so that the phrase is now anachronistic. Long-term research cited by economic historian Gavin Wright of Stanford University shows that educational integration in the South has produced positive economic results for African Americans, including increases in "graduation rates, test scores, earnings and adult health status, while reducing the probability of incarceration."

That's the good news. "One generation removed from the civil rights movement, we went from a country where a majority of the people believe in racial hierarchy, believed in the idea that there was one type of person who was fully deserving of citizenship, to a country where a majority of people reject that idea," says Sheryll Cashin, a Georgetown law professor and former clerk for Supreme Court Justice Thurgood Marshall. "Because of the civil rights movement, we became a country where a majority of people really embrace the idea of equality as an American ideal. It's seen as un-American to be discriminatory or racist. That's a major achievement, despite the fact that we still have inequality."

A LEGACY AT RISK

In a report issued in 2013, the National Urban League used the mark of 50 years since the March on Washington to measure the state of black America. In terms of education, the league notes that the high-school completion gap has closed by 57 points, the number of African Americans in college has tripled, and there are now five college graduates for every one in 1963. When it comes to standards of living, the percentage of African Americans living in poverty has fallen 23 points (the figure for black children is 22%), and homeownership among blacks has increased by 14%.

Then there are the all-too-familiar failures. "In the past 50 years," the Urban League reports, "the black-white income gap has only closed by 7 points (now at 60%). The unemployment-rate gap has only closed by 6 points (now at 52%)." (Only at 100% will the gap have disappeared.) Overall, the racial unemployment ratio is unchanged since 1963, at "about 2-to-1—regardless of education, gender, region of the country or income level." These numbers, as well as enduring inequalities in the criminal-justice system and the recent Supreme Court ruling on voting rights, suggest that neither the march nor the movement is really done.

This Is Our Hope *King and his lieutenants meet with Kennedy just after the march on Aug. 28, 1963.*

The end of Jim Crow did not mark the beginning of what John Lewis, since 1986 a congressman from Atlanta, calls "the beloved community"—a philosophical ideal of a world that transcends racial, ethnic, economic and gender barriers and is suffused by love. "Citizenship and equality are broader conceptions" than civil rights alone, says Darrell Miller, a professor at Duke Law School. "The civil rights movement was about ending segregation but also about being able to enjoy the fruits of being an equal citizen in all aspects of life, both public and private."

On that August Wednesday, on the steps of the Lincoln Memorial—the spot on which King stood is marked there now, a sacred slab hidden in plain sight in the middle of the capital of the most powerful nation the world has ever known—King drew from Scripture as he joined the ranks of the founders. In the beginning of the Republic, men dreamed big but failed to include everyone in that dream, limiting liberty largely to white men. Speaking in 1963, King brilliantly argued for the expansion of the founders' vision—nothing more, but surely nothing less. In doing so, a preacher from the South summoned a nation to justice and won his place in the American pantheon. "I have a dream that one day every valley shall be exalted, every hill and every mountain shall be made low. The rough places will be made plain, and the crooked places will be made straight. And the glory of the Lord shall be revealed, and all flesh shall see it together." He paused, then pressed on: "This is our hope. This is the faith that I will go back to the South with. With this faith we will be able to hew out of the mountain of despair a stone of hope." Transforming that hope into history remains the work at hand, this year and always. —WITH REPORTING BY MAYA RHODAN

CHAPTER FOUR

WE WERE THERE

THEY PLANNED AND ORGANIZED, LED AND INSPIRED:
FROM HARRY BELAFONTE AND JOAN BAEZ TO JOHN LEWIS
AND JULIAN BOND, 17 PARTICIPANTS IN THE MARCH ON
WASHINGTON RECALL THAT HISTORIC DAY

INTERVIEWS BY KATE PICKERT PHOTOGRAPHS BY MARCO GROB

John Lewis *'I grew up hearing Dr. King. The first
time I heard his voice, I was 15 years old.'*

HARRY BELAFONTE

Singer and activist

At the end of the Second World War, those of us who had participated in that conflict were under the impression that if we were triumphant over fascism and the Nazis, the men and women who returned from that conflict would be celebrated and honored by our nation. Many of us went off to that war and didn't have the right to vote. Many of us went off to that war and didn't have the right to participate in the American Dream. We didn't really think about this thing as a dream until Dr. King articulated it.

HANK THOMAS

Freedom Rider

We did not see this as simply a civil rights issue. It was a human rights issue. We were then beginning to connect our struggle with the struggles of people all over the world and especially the struggles in Africa, and it took some people a little bit aback that we would say we are fighting for our freedom. Because as far as most Americans were concerned—most white Americans—how can you connect segregation here with the totalitarianism and the dictatorships of Europe? To me it was the same thing. And we were saying to the world: This land of great opportunity, this land of liberty has an asterisk beside it. It is a land of freedom for everybody else except black people. This great March on Washington was our way of calling attention to it.

BELAFONTE: As a kid, there was not much I could aspire to, because the achievement of black people in spaces of power and rule and governance was not that evident, and therefore we were diminished in the way we thought we could access power and be part of the American fabric. We who came back from this war having expectations and finding that there were none to be

harvested were put upon to make a decision. We could accept the status quo as it was beginning to reveal itself with these oppressive laws still in place. Or, as had begun to appear on the horizon, stimulated by something Mahatma Gandhi of India had done, we could start this quest for social change by confronting the state a little differently. Let's do it nonviolently, let's use passive thinking applied to aggressive ideas, and perhaps we could overthrow the oppression by making it morally unacceptable.

RACHELLE HOROWITZ

March on Washington transportation director

A. Philip Randolph, the leader of the Brotherhood of Sleeping Car Porters and the dean of civil rights leaders, had initially called for a march in 1941. He postponed that march because Franklin Roosevelt gave him partially what he wanted in an Executive Order. Randolph never stopped dreaming and knowing that he had to have one.

BOB ZELLNER

Field secretary, Student Nonviolent Coordinating Committee

The feeling was that after 1961 and '62— those really tremendous years of a lot of action, starting in Greensboro, North Carolina, with the lunch-counter sit-ins, followed the next spring by the Freedom Rides—it was really kicking the movement into a new gear beyond the more passive but tremendously courageous boycott of the buses in Montgomery. It was a new phase of the movement. And there was a feeling that we would not be able to break Mississippi. We would not be able to break the Deep South. That March on Washing-

Harry Belafonte *'For us, each step of the way was a struggle with identity.'*

ton in '63 was to be the culmination of all of this intense organizing and bring the country to a realization that it has to not be a regional battle. It has to not be a young people's battle. It really has to be a moral crusade for the country.

HOROWITZ: Bayard Rustin was a civil rights activist who had played an instrumental role in developing the whole concept of nonviolence as protest action. He himself had been arrested about 20 times. He believed very deeply in something that A. Philip Randolph also believed in, and that is that the struggle for freedom in the United States had to eventually move to Washington, D.C., that it had to move to the center of power, to where the president and the Congress were—that no matter how many demonstrations took place in Montgomery and in Birmingham and places all around the South, until you could change the central government and have it legislate for all of the country, significant things wouldn't happen.

Randolph's contribution to the civil rights movement was a belief in mass action. Bayard added an organizer's ability, a concept of the strategy of mass action and also of nonviolence. He had a mind that went to every aspect of organization. No aspect of organizing was too small, and nothing was too large. He would worry about the kinds of sandwiches that would be there, the nature of the sound system, how one dealt with the president of the United States.

Clockwise from upper left: **Rachelle Horowitz** *'I was about 16 years old when Emmett Till was lynched.'* **Bob Zellner** *'My father was in the Klan, and my grandfather was in the Klan.'* **Doris Derby** *'I was a member of the NAACP youth chapter when I was 16.'* **Hank Thomas** *'I was one of the original Freedom Riders.'*

JOHN LEWIS

Chairman, Student Nonviolent Coordinating Committee, 1963–66; U.S. congressman from Georgia

I remember so well the first meeting that we had with President Kennedy in the Oval Office of the White House. We told him we were going to have a march on Washington, and you could tell by the body language of the president, he didn't like the idea of a march on Washington. He said, in effect, If you bring all these people to Washington, won't there be violence and chaos and disorder?

BELAFONTE: The conversation that I had with the White House and with the Justice Department was to say, Look, you know, this will not erupt into violence regardless of what J. Edgar Hoover and others say they see in our mix. We have a very solid group of citizens here. And part of that image was that the most trusted of our citizens, the most highly profiled, the most revered as celebrity will be there. So you'll have Burt Lancaster, and you'll have Paul Newman, and you'll have Marlon Brando and people like James Baldwin and other writers, and Lena Horne.

HOROWITZ: At the beginning of the march, when it was in its planning stage, Bayard started to get a series of letters from people who were friends of civil rights—senators. The letters all had the same theme. They went, "Dear Bayard, We really think that passage of the civil rights bill is the most important thing. We have supported the struggle for freedom. But have you considered the difficulties of having a march on Washington? Will there be enough toilets for the people there? Will there be enough water fountains?" Bayard eventually called them latrine letters. And while we laughed about them, he took them seriously. So we rented toilets, and we rented fountains so that people could drink water.

DORIS DERBY
Volunteer, Student Nonviolent
Coordinating Committee

Our committee met every week, and we said, O.K., what do we need to move this really large group of people from all over, to bring them in? We needed public relations. We needed to have a medical corps of nurses and doctors on hand. We needed to have porta-potties, arrange transportation. Once we had charter buses, regular buses coming in—what's going to happen to those? Where are people going to park?

HOROWITZ: It was a massive amount of phone calling, getting cards ready to be mailed, negotiations with various bus companies. Then we turned to trains and airplanes. Eventually we tried to charter everything that was charterable. We tried very much to help those people who were coming long distances to get trains for them. We actually had to raise a lot of money for that, because it was expensive and it was a Wednesday. It meant people had to take a day off from work. So we did a lot of fundraising. And we had what we called Freedom Trains from the South, which involved some negotiations with the Southern Railway.

ROBERT AVERY
March on Washington volunteer

I just turned 15 at the time, and there were a lot of things that were going on, of course, in the South, with demonstrations and the marches and picketing. But there was this great march they kept talking about that was going to happen in D.C., and myself and two other guys, we were sitting there talking about it, and we wanted to go. But of course we didn't have the money to catch the bus. So one of the guys said, Well, let's hitchhike. I looked at the other guy, and I said, Oh, yeah, that's great, let's do that—because we thought he

was just talking, and the more we talked, we realized he was serious.

BELAFONTE: We had Broadway shutting down, and we had large delegations of artists and celebrities coming from New York and from Boston and other places. It was not just in the world of cinema and theater. We had a lot of musical artists and record artists.

HOROWITZ: It is also a mark of Bayard's commitment to nonviolence and his organizing ability that at some point he realized that New York City policemen were required to carry their guns 24 hours a day. He said, Nobody is bringing a gun to this march. And he went to see Mayor Wagner or whoever the police authority was, and for that one day, New York City policemen were allowed to leave their guns home. The Justice Department also offered him the Army, the police, anything he wanted. And he said, No, if you want to do anything here, keep your troops on the periphery of the crowd and keep them watching for counterdemonstrators. We will monitor ourselves. You worry about provocateurs, racists, Klan members.

JULIAN BOND
Co-founder, Student Nonviolent
Coordinating Committee

The city of Washington almost went crazy. They canceled all elective surgery. They put surgeons and doctors on full time, waiting for something bad to happen. They put policemen on 18-hour shifts. They just went out of the way to prepare for what they thought would be some kind of massive riot. They couldn't imagine this many black people coming together without some awful, awful disturbance in the streets.

Maxine Allen Johnson Wood *'I could not believe that I had a chance to be a part of it.'*

The Hollywood Delegation *En route to the Lincoln Memorial: First row, from left: Charlton Heston, Julie Robinson and Harry Belafonte. Second row: James Garner, Diahann Carroll, Paul Newman. Third row: Anthony Franciosa, Marlon Brando*

HOROWITZ: Somebody at the National Council or the Red Cross said that the sandwiches had to be peanut butter and jelly. And Bayard came back to a staff meeting, and he said, O.K., we're writing this manual, and we have to tell people to bring peanut-butter-and-jelly sandwiches, no mayonnaise. Somebody said, But Bayard— And he said, This is not debatable! It became this sine qua non. Clearly what everybody was worried about was that you didn't want egg salad and mayonnaise spoiling on the road and people getting sick.

AVERY: We were there a week ahead of time, so they put us to work. Our job was to put together those signs. All of those signs that you see in the film clips—it was our job to staple them and put them together, then take them over to the parade grounds and unload them. I would imagine I probably touched every last one of those signs in some fashion or form. We probably put together, I don't know, 10,000 or more before we got to the parade ground. And of course, that morning people started coming in, and those signs were gone in a few minutes, and we had to get to work again putting more signs together.

BELAFONTE: In my instruction to my fellow artists when we met several times discussing strategy for what to do, I said, The more we can find ourselves in the heart of the people gathered at the event, the more we are seen and identified with the everyday citizen, the more we are all linking arms together, not just celebrity to celebrity but a truck driver, a dentist or a housewife, and we're all linking arms together, the more powerful that imagery becomes. My task was to make sure that we salt-and-peppered

Julian Bond *'Our parents, of course, said, don't get arrested, don't go to jail.'*

the afternoon into the early evening to look that way.

THOMAS: We were there to guide people, tell them where to go, what were the gathering points for the march, because obviously the vast majority of people had never been in D.C. before. So we had to direct them. A very large percentage of them came by bus, but there were other people who drove their automobiles. It was a question of showing them where to go in, how to get to the reflecting pool, into the Lincoln Memorial and to be of assistance to them in case we'd have any medical emergencies. That was primarily my job and the job of the marshals. We all owned distinctive armbands so people knew who we were.

I think it was about 7 o'clock that morning when we took our stations, and we didn't see anybody, and then within the next hour, people started pouring in, and it was just a wonderful sight.

AVERY: I don't really think they expected that many people. The word around the office was, when we were putting the signs together, If you get 35,000 or so, you're going to be O.K.

LEWIS: We came across Constitution Avenue, coming from the Senate side going down to the bottom of the hill, and we looked toward Union Station. There was a sea of humanity coming from Union Station, and the people were already marching, and it was like saying, There go my people. Let me catch up with them.

HOROWITZ: The chairmen were up on Capitol Hill meeting with the leaders of the House and Senate, and people at the Washington Monument had decided they were ready to go to the Lincoln Memorial. They formed lines, and they began to march, singing,

Joan Baez '*Speak truth to power. It's a Quaker expression. We felt that we could do that, and you know, we still can.*'

Rachel Robinson '*The lesson is not to stop, not to give up, not to believe that this is a postracist period. I don't buy that notion.*'

and an orderly march began spontaneously to the Lincoln Memorial so that by the time the march chairmen came, somebody had to stop the march, and they had to be put in front of what was really not the front of the line, just so they could lead it.

NAN ORROCK
March on Washington attendee;
Georgia state senator
It was an incredible experience being in a gathering of that size. It just felt like we were part of a glacier moving down the avenue.

AVERY: I became a participant like everybody else once the march started. Hey, if you need a sign, you've got to go put your own sign together—we're gone.

LEWIS: You saw signs from all over America: political signs, religious signs. People representing different faiths. Churches from the heart of the Midwest, the far West. People coming from all over the country to bear witness, to participate. Many of the people were well dressed. It was like going to church or temple or synagogue. People then, when they went out for a protest, they dressed up.

BOND: The interracial nature of the crowd is remarkable. You look at these pictures, and you see this is not a black crowd. This is black and white people. This is Americans saying, I don't like segregation. I want it to stop.

RACHEL ROBINSON
Widow of Jackie Robinson; founder of the
Jackie Robinson Foundation
The spirit in the whole setting was so exciting, so positive, so hopeful that something was going to happen. We felt very enthusiastic about everything. We were happy to wait and find a seat, and delighted when we found a seat up front so we could see the procedure and we could hear the speeches. It turned out to be an extraordinary experience for all of us—for the children and for Jack and I—because we had never worked on anything of that magnitude or seen that kind of support for equal opportunities, which is what we had been hoping for for many years.

LEWIS: I was 23 years old at the time. I remember A. Philip Randolph introduced me as he had introduced others. He stood and said, "I now present to you young John Lewis, the national chairman of the Student Nonviolent Coordinating Committee." I stood up, and I said to myself, This is it. I looked to my right: I saw hundreds and thousands of young people, many of the young volunteers of the Student Nonviolent Coordinating Committee. I looked to my left, and I saw many young people, young men, in the trees trying to get a better view of the podium. I looked straight out. And I started speaking.

It was an unbelievable feeling to see hundreds and thousands of people, black and white, sitting together, cheering. Many young people, men, women, they're taking off their shoes and putting their feet into the water to cool off. It was a hot day. It was very hot in Washington on Aug. 28, 1963.

JOAN BAEZ
Singer and activist
I remember it was hot. I remember what I was wearing. I remember singing. And I remember that ocean of people. I'd never seen anything like that. I remember the electricity in the air.

Peter Yarrow *'Music had become the soundtrack of the American conscience.'*

PETER YARROW
Singer and activist

We sang "If I Had a Hammer." They knew it, and they sang. And the moment was created not by the three of us in a performance but by a quarter of a million people gathering together and singing with us and saying, This moment belongs to us together. That's what singing together can do.

BELAFONTE: On the platform when these highly profiled, successful artists performed, it wasn't just that they were sympathetic and very much involved in the ideals of the struggle, it was that that's who they really were. They were artists, and they were superstars, and you could be both a powerfully received force and you can say the right thing. You can have a moral point of view.

BOND: I was giving Coca-Colas to the movie stars, and I can remember till my dying day giving a Coca-Cola to Sammy Davis Jr. and he said, Thanks, kid.

YARROW: Joyful doesn't really describe it for me. It was like the physicalization of love. It was ecstatic perhaps, but it was not giddy and silly or "let's have a good time." It was a far deeper kind of joy. It went beyond joy. It was hard to describe, but it was the antithesis of fear, and it propelled us all into another channel in our lives.

ORROCK: I was overwhelmed with the sense that I was in the presence of courage. So often you read about courage in books. To

Clockwise from upper left: **Robert Avery** '*I hitchhiked from Gaston, Ala., to Washington, D.C.*' **Marcus Garvey Wood** '*It seemed to me that the spirit of God came upon him.*' **Bob Adelman** '*I felt, this is history, and I should, as best I can, record it.*' **Nan Orrock** '*I'm the product of parents from the Deep South. I went to segregated schools.*'

be face to face and side by side with people who had made profound decisions to put at risk their own personal safety, their job, their home, the ability to support their family to go up in the face of the police-state atmosphere of the Deep South in order to get change was an overwhelming thought to me—the raw courage of people, to face police jailing you and beating you to the ground for the right to vote. So that was an overwhelming thing. I was so moved to think of the courage that it took for the people I was marching with to do what they were doing with their lives in very dangerous places, breaking the color line.

THOMAS: I was 21 years old, and I had this tremendous responsibility of helping to get this thing done. By the time the program started, I couldn't get as close to the Lincoln Memorial as I wanted to, because I had a job to do. Our job was to keep walking around, make sure there are no problems, because we knew of some of the things the FBI had done in the civil rights movement, putting in an agent or provocateurs.

MAXINE ALLEN JOHNSON WOOD
March on Washington attendee

Many of the speakers were people whose names were familiar, but you never would get the chance to see them. You're talking 50 years ago, so we didn't have the prominence of media. There wasn't any instant replay or quick exposure. So when you saw names like Harry Belafonte—he was listed as one of those speakers—or you saw the names of the civil rights leaders, and there were many of them who spoke before Martin Luther King, you were proud to be there and glad to be there.

MARCUS GARVEY WOOD
Seminary classmate of King's

I just felt for King as he sat there waiting to be introduced. I knew that the way they listened

Baez at the Podium *'I remember what I was wearing. I remember singing. And I remember that ocean of people. I'd never seen anything like that.'*

to people who were making speeches in rallies like this one, there was always somebody in the background trailing that speech with printed material. And I knew that somebody had a pencil following every word to see whether King would make a mistake or not repeat what he had placed there on paper. And I couldn't get to him to wink my eye or say to him, "Mike"—as we called him during the days of seminary—"come on, come on, you can do it, you can do it, you can do it."

CLARENCE B. JONES
Speechwriter for King

A lot of care and thought was given as to the kind of speech that he should give. We knew that people were coming from all over the country, and they were looking for political leadership. They were looking for direction, particularly after Birmingham. Black fury had broken out in 36 states and over 200 cities, and people were coming. So we felt that Dr. King's role was to give them political direction and moral reaffirmation of the validity of our struggle.

Now, among his advisers, there were those who were suggesting, as Ralph Abernathy would say, Martin, people are coming to the March on Washington because they're coming to hear you preach!

MARCUS WOOD: When we were in seminary together, King would walk around the hall preaching. He had more experience in preaching than some of us, although I was nine years older than he was and pastoring a small church in West Virginia. But when he became very popular, he called us together and said, You all must stick by me, for I am going to dismantle this society. And we would jokingly say to him, King, if you try to dismantle this society that we're in now, somebody's going to shoot you. Somebody's going to bring you down, because society is so ingrained with segregation. The culture

has been born into segregation, and therefore it's not going to change.

JONES: I'm standing on the platform about 50 feet behind him, and he is introduced by A. Philip Randolph in this sonorous voice: "At this time, I have the honor to present to you the moral leader of our nation. I have the pleasure to present to you Dr. Martin Luther King Jr." The place goes crazy! I mean it's just like an explosion of approval. I'm looking at the audience as he's looking at them. Then as he's speaking, Mahalia Jackson, who had performed earlier on the program and who was his favorite gospel singer, interrupted him: "Tell 'em about the dream, Martin. Tell 'em about the dream."

I'm watching him from the back. He takes the text of the speech that he was reading, and he moves it to the side of the lectern. And then he grabs both sides of the lectern, and I say to the person standing next to me—whoever that was—I said, These people don't know it, but they're about ready to go to church.

BOB ADELMAN
Photographer

I think it's when he starts to talk about the dream that, like the greatest jazz musician, he just does an incredible solo.

BOND: His ability to summon from his memory and deviate from his written text was just remarkable to me. I make speeches all the time. I can't do without a piece of paper in front of me. But he could just draw these ideas, draw these images, paint these pictures. It was just a remarkable performance. I've never seen anything as good as this ever, and I doubt if I ever will.

Jerome Smith *'It was a procession of church. It was never, ever a march. It was a congregation that was answering the call.'*

Pocket watch given to event organizer Bayard Rustin by King;
Washington Monument platform pass

JEROME SMITH

Freedom Rider

You know, at bottom, Dr. King is a musician. And if he was reciting the telephone book, the rhythms and transition to phrasing would bring you to an emotional acceptance.

AVERY: I get goose bumps when I think about it. He was at his best. That's all I can say. But in his talking, and my mind wandering back to what I had been through that summer, and when he started talking about his children, I felt like, Wow, he's talking about me. He's talking to me.

ROBINSON: We listened very carefully to the words as if they were almost like instructions. We all wanted to do something, and we wanted to have goals that we were going to work toward. And the speech gave a lot of ideas in terms of that. It wasn't just a spiritual thing. It was also very informative and instructive. We were looking for leadership, and he was offering it.

BOND: What was really wonderful about the March on Washington is this is the first time most white people watching this on television had ever seen Dr. King give a full speech. They'd heard snippets and pieces of his oratory, but he was such a wonderful speaker, and he made an argument for the rightness of black protest.

HOROWITZ: I think the biggest expenditure made was for the sound system. I remember Bayard being absolutely adamant that everybody on that Mall had to hear every minute of every speech. And it's sort of amazing to think about that now if you think that Dr. King gave that speech without a Jumbotron—250,000 people in the trees down the Mall watched him and listened to him.

MAXINE WOOD: That "I have a dream"—to hear it, initially, was an important experience. To hear him give that message made you believe you did have a dream, and it was very inspiring. A lot of people probably had not focused

Cap worn at the march by Roy Wilkins, then executive secretary of the NAACP; armband worn by event marshals; guitar played by Baez at the march

on those possibilities. We live in realities, but the image that he gave was a future.

JONES: If you listen to the speech carefully—and this is important as we reflect now 50 years back—if you listen to the syntax of his reference to the dream, he does not speak in the present tense. He speaks in the future tense. He's speaking in his hope and belief in America. "I have a dream that my four little children will one day live in a nation where they will not be judged by the color of their skin but by the content of their character." Future tense.

Dr. King's speech at the March on Washington was an affirmation of his prophetic belief that America had the capacity to be the best that it could be. The "I Have a Dream" speech was a summons, a call, to the collective conscience of America, that we can be better than this. We can be better than this!

BAEZ: There are some times when you know something is going to be historic. I was just

at Woodstock—went back and revisited the place—and we knew that. And certainly by the time this few hundred thousand people had gathered, you knew that whatever it was you were going to say or do was going to be recorded as part of history.

ADELMAN: When I hear that speech—I mean this is what, 50 years later?—I still cry. It's so extraordinary, but when he finished speaking, I really had a profound sense that it was now almost inevitable. Such a force had been unleashed that history was moving. He had spoken in front of Lincoln's likeness, and I said, This is going to happen.

SMITH: It was a ritual—it was a procession of church. It was never, ever a march. It was a congregation that was answering the call.

YARROW: It changed the course of our lives. It gave us not only an internal sense of what we believed in being validated, but it gave us a sense of the community of commitment that was to change America. Not only in terms of African Americans, but to be able to say that ordinary human beings can gather together in large numbers, and if they gather together with heart and strength, they can change the course of history.

ORROCK: Think about this: The average white kid, to the degree they thought about it, we were taught all about democracy. You're taught all about what we stand for, one nation, and undivided, liberty and justice for all, all those words we'd been taught. But those words applied to the white people. And we would all chant them and cite them and read them and study them and hear them from our teachers and not face this enormous contradiction that this doesn't apply to everybody. Everybody's not equal. Everybody can't vote. Everybody can't get a job when they apply for one, can't live where they want to, doesn't have the same shot at raising a family with a future.

BOND: If the goal was to normalize the civil rights movement, then the goal was achieved. Not everybody in the country said, Oh, I understand. But many people then understood what they had not understood before, that black people were dissatisfied, that the segregation system they faced was untenable. It could not be maintained, and it had to be changed.

BELAFONTE: In the end, the day was a complete win-win. The Kennedys heaved a huge sigh of relief that there was not one act of violence. And to see at the end everybody singing "We Shall Overcome" and all the arms linked—we've said it often, but it's worth saying as often as necessary: there wasn't a dry eye in the house. And it was all of America. All of it. You went through that crowd and you couldn't find any type missing, any gender, any race, any

religion. It was America at its most transformative moment.

AVERY: The closing was—I couldn't believe it. I'd been there for a whole week, and we worked in the office, we'd done all these things, and now this great march—it was just unbelievable.

THOMAS: It brought our struggle to the attention of the world. That was the most important impact that I thought it had. But insofar as me personally? I was going to continue to work. It was a motivating factor, but it just added to the amount of motivation that I already had.

ORROCK: Years later, I got a very special letter from my mother. Years later—after I'd been very involved and a full-time civil rights worker and always talking to my mother about what needed to change and why I was doing this—she wrote me a letter that she was really proud that I had understood this long before she did and long before most people like us had understood it, and that I had stood with Dr. King and with the civil rights movement, and that I had done the right thing, and that she was very proud of me.

LEWIS: After Dr. King had spoken, we went back down to the White House. President Kennedy invited us back down, and he stood in the door to the Oval Office and greeted each one of us. He was like a proud beaming father that everything had gone so well. He said to each one of us as he shook our hand, You did a good job, you did a good job. And when he got to Dr. King, he said, And you had a dream.

Clarence B. Jones *'This country owes a debt to Martin Luther King Jr. that can never, ever be repaid.'*

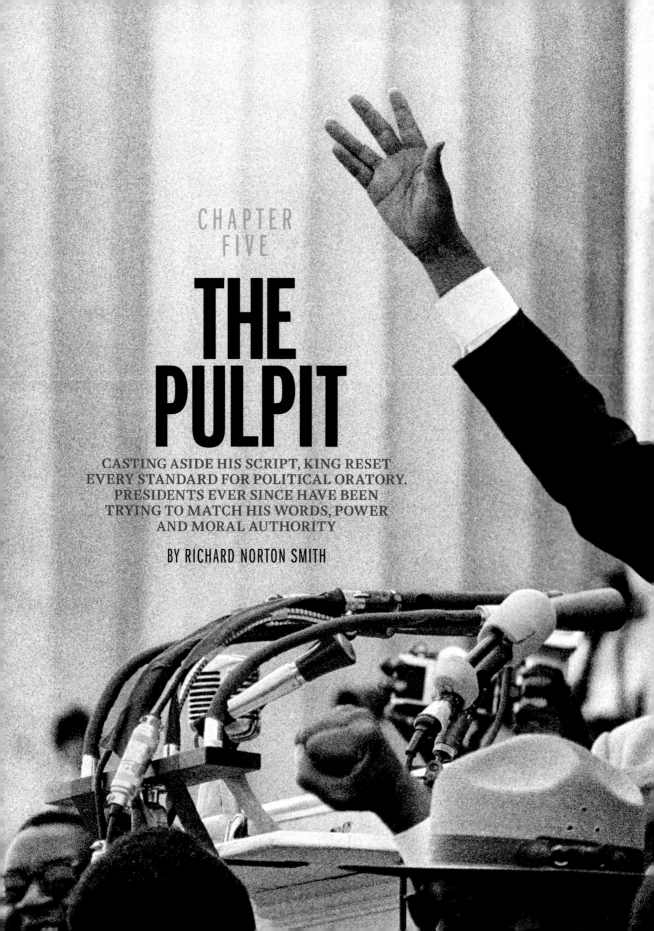

CHAPTER
FIVE

THE PULPIT

CASTING ASIDE HIS SCRIPT, KING RESET
EVERY STANDARD FOR POLITICAL ORATORY.
PRESIDENTS EVER SINCE HAVE BEEN
TRYING TO MATCH HIS WORDS, POWER
AND MORAL AUTHORITY

BY RICHARD NORTON SMITH

Free at Last *King on the steps of the Lincoln Memorial as the speech ends. Behind the scenes, one of President Kennedy's advance men stood ready to pull the plug on the sound system.*

ON AUGUST 28, 1963, no one followed Martin Luther King Jr.'s oratorical

tour de force more closely than the president of the United States. "He's damn good," murmured John F. Kennedy as King's triumphant image faded from the television screen. Left unmentioned was King's introduction on the steps of the Lincoln Memorial as "the moral leader of the nation."

But it must have stung so astute a student of presidential history as Kennedy. Sooner or later, fairly or not, every occupant of the Oval Office is judged by his use of the bully pulpit, invented by Theodore Roosevelt to shame purveyors of tainted meat, promote simplified spelling, and trumpet the conservation of nature in opposition to a money lust recognizable to any viewer of CNBC's *American Greed*. Since then, a century's worth of richly symbolic gestures—from T.R.'s White House dinner invitation to Booker T. Washington, the first of his race to be so honored, to Barack Obama's painfully personal testimony about racial profiling in the wake of the Trayvon Martin verdict—have demonstrated a president's capacity to foster change through his moral advocacy.

Appearing briefly in the White House press room on July 19, 2013, Obama supplied the latest teachable moment in the nation's 400-year seminar on race. An obvious reluctance to let the issue define his presidency only lent added weight to Obama's comments. So did their juxtaposition against the 50th anniversary of the 1963 March on Washington for Jobs and Freedom. To its organizers, the first great Washington protest of a transformative decade was as much about unfinished business as unkept promises. Movement veterans like A. Philip Randolph and Roy Wilkins had vivid memories of an even earlier demonstration scheduled for July 1, 1941, and aborted at the last minute when FDR issued Executive Order 8802, which desegregated the nation's war industries and established a Fair Employment Practices Committee to monitor workplace discrimination.

The alternative—100,000 black protesters marching to the Lincoln Memorial—held scant appeal for a president whose congressional prospects rested with Southern Democrats committed to American apartheid. Reserving his powers of persuasion for the threat posed by fascist dictators in Europe and Asia, Roosevelt tossed the hand grenade of civil rights to his outspoken wife Eleanor. When the Daughters of the American Revolution denied the celebrated contralto Marian Anderson the use of Constitution Hall on account of her race, Mrs. Roosevelt resigned her membership in the group. She gave her blessing to local activists who were seeking a highly symbolic change of venue.

April 9, 1939, dawned cold and blustery in the nation's capital, though it didn't prevent a crowd of 75,000 dressed in their Easter finery from assembling before the Lincoln Memorial to hear Anderson's emotionally charged "My Country, 'Tis of Thee." Among the millions listening via radio was a 10-year-old preacher's son in Atlanta named Martin Luther King Jr. In a high-school speaking competition he won several years later, King described the concert as "a new baptism of liberty, equality and fraternity." The same event redefined a monument whose mixed message reflected a national habit, where race was concerned, of editing the past to avoid discomforting the present. At its formal unveiling in 1922, former president William Howard Taft described Abraham Lincoln's Greek Doric temple as "a shrine at which all can worship."

Yet the throng to which he addressed those words was rigidly segregated. So was the history being commemorated. Tuskegee Institute president Robert R. Moton had his remarks edited lest he offend Lincoln's son, President Warren Harding and other dignitaries assembled to pay homage to the 16th president—for what? Architect Henry Bacon spelled it out in the memo-

On their feet *Midway through his remarks, King abandoned his text. The reaction was tumultuous.*
PHOTOGRAPH © FLIP SCHULKE

rial's epigraph: "In this temple as in the hearts of the people for whom he saved the Union the memory of Abraham Lincoln is enshrined forever." To African Americans, however, starting with Frederick Douglass, preserving the Union took second place to ending slavery. Their Lincoln was found in the second Inaugural Address justifying the war, and more than 600,000 related deaths, as divine retribution for the crime of human bondage.

'A GREAT CHANGE IS AT HAND'

After 1939, the brooding man of marble supplied a backdrop to both presidents and protesters as they prodded the conscience of white America. In June 1947, Harry Truman became the first chief executive to appear before the NAACP when he addressed 10,000 of the group's members from the memorial's steps. That Truman—a product of small-town Missouri who was known to employ the N word in private conversation—should risk splitting his party by desegregating the armed forces and sending the first civil rights message to Congress since Reconstruction lent his actions a moral majesty consistent with Lincoln's outgrowing of the racist society that had produced him. That Truman also embraced civil rights because he couldn't hope to win the 1948 election without black votes simply married pragmatism to principle.

Dwight Eisenhower's hidden-hand style of leadership avoided rhetorical flourishes. Though accompanied by the requisite Oval Office address, his 1957 deployment of Army troops to escort nine black children into a formerly segregated high school in Little Rock, Ark., spoke for itself. Three years later, John Kennedy's impromptu phone call to Coretta Scott King expressing concern over her husband's jailing for his part in an Atlanta protest may well have supplied Kennedy's razor-thin margin over Richard Nixon in their race for the White House. Yet civil rights went unmentioned in Kennedy's Inaugural Address, the new president giving priority to Cold War dangers. To be sure, the Kennedy administration sent federal marshals to protect Freedom Riders who challenged segregation on interstate transport. And in 1962 a plainly frustrated JFK mobilized federal troops so that James Meredith could attend the University of Mississippi. As history accelerated in the first months of 1963, pictures rather than words aroused a nation's conscience. From the front pages of newspapers they spilled onto television screens by the millions: jaw-dropping images of black children in Birmingham, Ala., savaged by high-powered water hoses and police dogs answerable to commissioner of public safety Eugene "Bull" Connor. At the White House, Kennedy said the pictures made him sick. He furtively lobbied Birmingham business executives to compromise with King and his Children's Crusade. When Alabama Governor George Wallace attempted on June 11 to keep two black students from enrolling at the University of Alabama in a confrontation staged for television, Kennedy's detachment crumbled. That night he went on the air with an improvised speech to rally support for a civil rights bill that had yet to be written. "Those who do nothing," the president told his audience, "are inviting shame, as well as violence. Those who act boldly are recognizing right, as well as reality."

In shedding the chrysalis of political calculation, Kennedy achieved his own profile in courage. Yet even then, fearing the impact on his re-election prospects, he initially held back from endorsing the proposed March on Washington. Why risk alienating potential supporters through tactics of intimidation? On the day of the march, John R. Lewis, the 23-year-old firebrand who was newly elected to lead the Student Nonviolent Coordinating Committee, saw his text purged of language upsetting to the white audience by march leaders, much as Robert Moton had in consecrating Lincoln's shrine four decades earlier.

King's speech concluding the day's program quickly assumed legendary status. "I have a dream," JFK said, greeting King as he arrived for a postmarch meeting in the Oval Office. The immediate political payoff was more disappointing. Senator Hubert Humphrey lamented that the march had failed to convert a single colleague to support civil rights legislation. Three months later, Kennedy's assassination conjured memories of another martyred president, succeeded by another Southerner named Johnson, whose white-supremacist dogma had set back by a hundred years the cause of racial justice. Determined to validate his presidency born of tragedy, Lyndon Johnson would employ the bully pulpit with heroic disregard for the political consequences. "There goes the South for a generation," Johnson reportedly observed in signing the landmark 1964 Civil Rights Act. It was a rare instance of Johnsonian understatement.

A year later, on a March Sabbath christened Bloody Sunday, 600 demonstrators demanding equal access to the voting booth assembled on the outskirts of Selma, Ala., where they were clubbed and teargassed by state troopers and local police. What followed was perhaps Johnson's finest hour. "What happened in Selma is part of a far larger movement which reaches into every section and state of America," he told a joint session of Congress. "It is the effort of American Negroes to secure for themselves the full blessings of American life. Their cause must be our cause too, because it is not just Negroes but really it is all of us who must overcome the crippling legacy of bigotry and injustice. And we *shall* overcome." Johnson's words that night moved King to tears. In the finest tradition of the bully pulpit, they illustrate the difference between a president who preaches at us and one who undertakes to explain us to ourselves. That said, the pulpit isn't what it used to be. Long gone are the days when a presidential address from the Oval Office automatically commanded a television audience of 70 million, countered only by the lonely voice of Eric Sevareid offering what the three television networks labeled instant analysis. Today President Obama is lucky to be seen in the cable universe, shouting into the wind of millions of self-appointed Sevareids tweeting their impressions of his speech as he delivers it.

Likewise consigned to memory are the Frank Capra–esque exploits of Ronald Reagan instigating a flood of calls to Capitol Hill, enough to shake loose dozens of Southern Democrats needed to pass his economic program. The fragmentation of the modern media guarantees it. So does the disappearance of Southern Democrats. These days the loyal opposition couldn't care less about jammed phones; they're too busy jamming the operations of government itself. Meanwhile Barack Obama, our putative instructor in chief, is ensnared in a political culture that defines success not as forging consensus but as preventing it. The president has been criticized for not employing his persuasive powers more forcefully. This sidesteps the question: How does a president persuade congregation members who have tuned him out, disputing his legitimacy and reserving their attention for those who reinforce their existing prejudices?

That is precisely what made the president's remarks following the Trayvon Martin verdict so compelling. In sharing bitter memories of car doors being locked in response to his mere presence, Obama offers a postmodern version of the bully pulpit. Less theatrical than T.R.'s bluster, less elegant than JFK's belated conversion to freedom as every American's birthright, less urgent than LBJ's moral imperative, Obama's parking-lot epiphany is as chillingly authentic as it is impossible to dismiss. Neither Kennedy nor King, this president appears less interested in directing a national conversation on race than in sparking interior dialogue, a discussion beginning not with his standing before Congress but with the rest of us figuratively staring into our mirrors.

Richard Norton Smith is a presidential historian and scholar-in-residence at George Mason University.

WHAT THE DREAM MEANS TO ME

I HAVE A DREAM TOO
MALALA YOUSAFZAI

Martin Luther King Jr. inspired millions of people, including me, to dream. His words—still so powerful after half a century—empower us to continue the journey to our destination of peace and equality. He was, of course, a great human-rights activist and leader. He stood up against segregation and inspired America to be a country for people of all colors and creeds. He raised his voice for freedom with honesty. He dreamed and changed the world with a few unforgettable, powerful words.

His legacy is that those words reached far beyond America's shores and far beyond the generation to whom he spoke. They are relevant today. They are relevant to me, a girl born almost 30 years after he died, from a country more than 7,000 miles away.

My dream is to see every child with a book and pen. I dream that every woman in the world will be treated with dignity and equality, fifty years on from his famous oration in Washington, D.C.

Yousafzai is a Pakistani activist.

WE'VE GOT TO KEEP MARCHING
JESSE JACKSON

In many ways, the March on Washington was a culmination of actions from Dec. 1, 1955, to Aug. 28, 1963. We were at the dawn of a new day, and it had taken daylight a long time to come. The essence of Dr. King's speech was not the dream; it was the broken promise.

We had been promised the accommodations of full citizenship, the right to vote. We had been promised equal protection under the law and equal opportunity. Yet in our quest for citizenship, the promise was broken.

The spirit at the march was that we were winning, and we were doing it together. Blacks, whites—we were a multiracial social-justice coalition. That was before we had the public accommodation and before we had the right to vote. But those victories were in sight.

We had this sense that we were winning; we were rising up. We had overcome fear. That speech was an early indication that if we keep marching, if we keep pushing, we're going to win this battle. It was a dawn-to-daylight speech, and we won.

Now we have the sense that we're at dusk, moving toward midnight. One thing we can learn from Dr. King is that the forces of equal protection should neither sleep nor slumber. We got the right to vote in 1870 after 200 years of slavery. In 1965 we got the Voting Rights Act, but in 2013 the Supreme Court eviscerated it. The struggle for democracy and equal protection will never be a past-tense discussion.

Jackson is a minister and civil rights activist.

NO GREATER MANIFESTO FOR AMERICA
THEODORE B. OLSON

Martin Luther King's "I Have a Dream" speech should be required reading for every American. Like the Declaration of Independence and the Gettysburg Address, it is an elegant, passionate and unforgettable distillation of the aspiration and inspiration of America. In just a few paragraphs, King expressed his anguish at unfulfilled

Man of the Hour *King shakes hands with the crowd at the March on Washington.*

promises, the urgency facing America to live up to its ideals, and his abiding faith that it could and would do so.

King pronounced the time for patience to have expired and shared his deeply rooted conviction that his dream would, at long last, coalesce. He made clear that the need for action was immediate and compelling, while exhorting blacks to renew their faith in America. There has been no greater reminder of what this nation held itself out to be and no greater plea for us to attain those ideals, no greater invocation of the spirit of Jefferson and Lincoln.
Olson is a Republican advocate for same-sex marriage.

TEETERING ON A TIGHTROPE
SHONDA RHIMES

I've known large parts of this speech by heart since before I could read. My father likes to quote the words of great men at the dinner table. King's definitely qualified.

To me, a child born in the '70s, the words of his speech seemed vaguely confusing. What was the fuss? King had a dream, and it came true: I held hands with the little white girl next door almost every day when I went out to play. As I got older, I came to realize that while King's dream had become something of a reality in small pockets of America, in the larger world it was more ethereal.

We are living in a strange time in terms of race in this country. We're teetering on a tightrope between greatness and madness. A man of color can be president of the United States. A man of color can be shot for wearing a hoodie. We haven't gotten to King's promised land. There's still work to be done.
Rhimes is a writer and producer.

A Multiethnic Sea *Marchers gathered in the shadow of the Washington Monument.*

KEEPING OUR PROMISE
MARCO RUBIO

A half-century has passed since Dr. Martin Luther King Jr. stood on the steps of the Lincoln Memorial to awaken our nation's conscience. His vision was simple yet profound: that America must fulfill the promise made in her founding documents by allowing every citizen to access their God-given rights.

Dr. King helped bring hope to men and women of all backgrounds who wished to contribute to American exceptionalism. That included immigrants like my parents, who made a new life here after coming from Cuba. They immigrated in 1956—the year Dr. King led the Montgomery bus boycott—and raised my siblings and me in the wake of his legacy, telling us our dreams were possible regardless of the circumstances of our births.

I have taken my own children to the Lincoln Memorial and shown them where Dr. King spoke to the unfulfilled promise of our nation. Standing in that place, I was filled with pride to know my children live in a nation where the cultural landscape is dramatically different from the one that Dr. King saw just 50 years before.

Dr. King reminded us that opportunity and freedom are American ideals, belonging to no singular demographic. His message and legacy must live all around us and his dream must continue to lead us as we move toward America's brightest days. *Rubio is a Republican senator from Florida.*

THE PATH FORWARD
JOHN CONYERS

I am proud to say that I owe my political career to the inspiration that came from Dr. Martin Luther King Jr.

I first met Dr. King and his wife Coretta

in the early 1960s. After the Supreme Court upheld the principle of "one person, one vote," Michigan was required to create a new congressional seat in Detroit, which I ran for in 1964. Thanks to the recommendation of my good friend Rosa Parks, I became the only congressional candidate ever endorsed by Dr. King.

I was proud to cast one of my very first votes in Congress for the Voting Rights Act of 1965. That document, along with the 1964 Civil Rights Act and the 1968 Fair Housing Act, is a crown jewel of our civil rights laws. They represent the very spirit of King's "I Have a Dream" speech (a phrase he first used in the Freedom March in Detroit, two months earlier).

Despite the historic election of our first African American president, the challenges remain daunting. In June the Supreme Court weakened the Voting Rights Act at a time when many states are adding onerous new voter-ID requirements. Affirmative action is under assault in the courts. Our schools are becoming resegregated. But these challenges are not insurmountable. Through a renewed commitment to the teachings of Dr. King, we must keep the struggle alive.
Conyers is a Democratic congressman from Michigan.

DARING TO DREAM
ELIJAH E. CUMMINGS
As I was growing up in a low-income family in Baltimore, my biggest exposures to the world beyond the borders of my community were my family's black-and-white TV, the movies I went to see and visiting relatives. From these glimpses I learned there were places we couldn't go, things we couldn't do and dreams we shouldn't have.

At age 9, I joined a group of children organized by local NAACP leaders in a march from the tiny "colored" wading pool to the

Olympic-size "white" pool a few blocks away. We marched under the threat of violence—not to change the world but because we wanted to swim. Dr. King's speech, delivered shortly after we integrated the pool, gave our march context and empowered me. I was just a kid, but even then I knew that things would have to change. His speech gave me the hope to believe that they would.
Cummings is a Democratic congressman from Maryland.

DREAMS OF DEMOCRACY
WANG DAN
When Dr. Martin Luther King Jr. gave his "I Have a Dream" speech, he must have known that very few people believed such a vision could come true. Nevertheless, he did not hesitate to stand up and speak. Throughout history, idealists have been willing to commit to dreams that seem impossible. But dreams are more powerful than doubt or violence. When I helped lead the peaceful student protest in Tiananmen Square in 1989, critics said our movement was doomed. The tanks rolled in and many people were killed. I am now in exile. But I know that our hopes for a democratic China will eventually be realized. History allowed Martin Luther King's dream to prevail. China also deserves to dream.
Wang is a Chinese democracy-movement leader.

VOICE TO THE VOICELESS
CHARLAYNE HUNTER-GAULT
As thousands stood on the Mall in Washington, D.C., I was sitting in a small office on West 43rd Street in New York City, where I was positioned to fulfill my own dream. Thanks to the work of some of those in the crowd—black professionals from Atlanta who moved to realize the promise of the Supreme Court decision outlawing school segregation—I was able to walk through the doors of a university, all-white

for 176 years, to prepare for a career I had dreamed of since childhood.

Now, three months after graduation, I was glued to a television screen at the *New Yorker*, where I had been given a job as an editorial assistant. On that August day, I unashamedly shed tears listening to John Lewis and Dr. King. I took to heart their words, vowing that I would use the realization of my dream to give voice to the voiceless and tell their stories in the pages of the *New Yorker* and wherever else the "lift of a driving dream" would take me. It is a promise I continue to try to fulfill. Thanks to the example of the tireless marchers in Washington, I try to "keep on keepin' on" and "don't feel no ways tired."
Hunter-Gault is a journalist.

A WAR OF MORALS
COLIN POWELL
I was in Vietnam in August 1963. I was not able to see or hear Dr. King's speech, and in those days the news to Vietnam traveled slowly. My wife Alma was in Birmingham with our infant son. During that ugly summer, my father-in-law stood guard to protect my family while I was fighting for our country 8,000 miles away.

I returned home to find America embroiled in a second Civil War, one led by Dr. King. It was a war of morals, righteousness and the aspirations of our Founding Fathers. The "I Have a Dream" speech held up a mirror for all Americans to look deeply into the spirit and soul of our country.

The "Dream" speech, along with the Civil Rights Act and Voting Rights Act that followed, finally broke the bonds of segregation and Jim Crow that had imprisoned our finest dreams. Not only were African Americans given a berth of freedom, but white America had a horrible burden removed from its back. Fifty years later, we have seen great progress. But we are not yet where

we need to be. Education, jobs, health care and good housing for all Americans must remain our goal. We all must work together if Dr. King's dream is to be fully realized.
Powell was U.S. Secretary of State from 2001 to 2005.

EDUCATION IS THE KEY
GEOFFREY CANADA
Fifty years ago, the No. 1 issue for African Americans was blatant discrimination. Due in part to Dr. King's powerful words, the country passed legislation that led us away from Jim Crow and moved us toward embracing our differences and seeing them as a source of strength.

Today, though, we still have a black-white achievement gap in education and deeply troubling statistics about incarceration, substance abuse and unemployment. They tell us Dr. King's dream has not been fully realized. Our country has come a long way in terms of civil rights, but we still have a long way to go.

Education is the key to achieving the dream. Our public-education system, the step up for so many Americans, is failing to prepare huge numbers of our children for the future. That threatens the dream for all of us.
Canada is president and CEO of the Harlem Children's Zone.

REMEMBERING BROTHER MARTIN
SONIA SANCHEZ
How to tell you about this aristocratic word sorcerer with a commoner's eye? How to make you hear our tears as he welcomed our souls and held our hearts in his hands? This Martin Luther King man was a *cante jondo*, a deep song of Africa. The South. The Americas.

He came toward us with the staccato speech and rhythm of the spirit. And his passion entered this American bloodstream. He no longer spoke for himself. Something began to move through him. He levitated

Congregants *Singer Lena Horne, a lifelong NAACP member, spoke, performed and listened that day.*

language and we wept, laughed, hummed till time stood still. He had summoned the *duende*, the spirit of all of our ancestors who had suffered and yet survived, and did it with dignity and grace and order and beauty.

He told us that we had affirmed life, that our eyes had abandoned death, defeat. That our feet were dancing silver.

In August 1963, we heard the thunder of angels.
Sanchez is an author and poet.

THERE IS STILL HOPE
MAYA ANGELOU

It was 50 years ago when the Rev. King had that dream and dared to say so, that little black children in Florida and in Mississippi and in Georgia and in South Carolina would stand with little white children and hold hands, that they themselves would dream the dream. What a dream. Can you imagine if we did not have this undergirded hate and racism, prejudices and sexism and ageism? If we were not crippled by these idiocies, can you imagine what our country would be like?

This is not to say we have not had progress—in fact, tremendous progress. After the lives and deaths of Martin Luther King Jr. and Malcolm X and the Kennedys and Fannie Lou Hamer, young people may say, You mean it is no better? But it is better.

There is still hope. If there were not, there would be no reason to get up in the morning. There is hope. Sometimes you need to be jarred into finding it, jarred into sharing it. I remember a statement of the Rev. King's that you ought to believe something in life, believe in something so fervently that you will stand up with it until the end of your days. I think we all have to believe that the day will come that we do not have to be saddled; we will not be crippled with all this idiocy. I hope for that. I am still working for it. I am still writing for that. I speak of that. I sing about that. I pray about that.
Angelou is an author and poet.

CHAPTER SIX

ECHOES OF A SUNDAY MORNING

**FIFTY YEARS AFTER THE BIRMINGHAM
BOMBING THAT KILLED FOUR GIRLS, THE
CITY SHOWS JUST HOW FAR IT HAS COME**

BY JON MEACHAM

Recognition *Last year the four girls who lost their lives in
the bombing at the 16th Street Baptist Church, at right, were
posthumously awarded a Congressional Gold Medal. From left:
McNair, Robertson, Collins and Wesley*

FOURTEEN-YEAR-OLD William Bell was getting ready for church when he

heard the blast. It was 10:22 a.m. on the morning of Sunday, Sept. 15, 1963, and the sound of the dynamite exploding at the 16th Street Baptist Church roared across Birmingham. The noise startled even the Bells, who lived nearly three miles away on Fifth Avenue Southwest in the city's Titusville neighborhood. Young Bell's father rushed him into the family car and they drove to the church, where they found chaos and tragedy: four young girls, Bell's contemporaries, had been massacred by a white supremacists' bomb: Denise McNair, 11; Carol Robertson, 14; Cynthia Wesley, 14; and Addie Mae Collins, 14. "Every individual in this town knew at least one of the girls or knew their families," Bell says. "Carol Robertson is a cousin of mine. That impacted our family. Denise McNair went to school with my brother. Her mother taught my brother. You felt it, the pain of it."

Fifty Septembers later, William Bell, now the mayor of Birmingham, presides over a city faced with the perennially complicated task of bearing witness to the past while simultaneously moving beyond it. The attack on the 16th Street Baptist Church was an act of terror and of martyrdom that stands as one of the great turning points in American history. Together with the August March on Washington, the September murder of the four little girls in what was known as "Bombingham" for its persistent racial violence opened the way for Lyndon Johnson's successful push for legislation in 1964 after the November assassination of President Kennedy.

September 15th was the annual "Youth Sunday" at the 16th Street church. The girls were gathering before the 11 a.m. service—a service they were to lead in the sanctuary. They were excited; it was a big day. They had just finished the day's Sunday School lesson in Mrs. Ella C. Demand's class (its title: "The Love That Forgives") and had adjourned to a lounge in the northeast corner of the building to prepare themselves for the main liturgy. Then the dynamite hidden by a group of Ku Klux Klansmen went off.

Tragically, the attack was only the most dramatic of many such hours of violence in the South in general and in Birmingham in particular in those years. The *New York Times* reported that there had been 50 unsolved bombings of African American property in the city since World War II, and the white power structure, from the governor to the mayor to the mass of white citizens, showed far too little interest in solving anything.

Yet there had been some hope a few months before. In June 1963, in reaction to the widespread police attacks on nonviolent protestors, including children, President Kennedy had delivered a remarkable speech from the Oval Office proposing civil rights legislation. "Now the time has come for this nation to fulfill its promise," Kennedy had said. "The events in Birmingham and elsewhere have so increased the cries for equality that no city or state or legislative body can prudently choose to ignore them. The fires of frustration and discord are burning in every city, North and South ... A great change is at hand, and our task, our obligation, is to make that revolution, that change, peaceful and constructive for all."

The forces of reaction were ready to strike, and strike they did. Medgar Evers of the NAACP was assassinated in Mississippi just hours after Kennedy's address. Alabama Governor George C. Wallace also took his "stand" in the schoolhouse door the day of the president's speech, fighting the integration of the University of Alabama. A canny politician, Wallace so believed in his defense of segregation that he was about to test the presidential waters

Mourning *Juanita Jones, center, comforts her sister, Maxine McNair, whose daughter Denise was one of the four young girls killed by the Klan's bomb.*

by putting his name on the Maryland Democratic ballot. The governor sensed that his flamboyant defiance of the federal government's attempts to enforce integration would play beyond Alabama—a sign that neither Kennedy's June speech nor the March on Washington had fundamentally changed long-held white views on race and power.

Then came the bombing. "There is a great deal of frustration and despair and confusion in the Negro community," Martin Luther King Jr. told Kennedy afterward. "And there is a feeling of being alone and not being protected. If you walk the street, you aren't safe. If you stay at home, you aren't safe—there's a danger of a bombing. If you're in church now, it isn't safe. So the Negro feels that everywhere he goes, if he remains stationary, he's in danger of some physical violence."

Kennedy was sympathetic but felt constrained. The most practical of men, he told King and others that he did not see how the deaths of the four little girls really altered the political calculus that prevented him from sending in federal troops or doing more than he was already doing in trying to move civil rights legislation through a reluctant Congress. "Now it's tough for the Negro community," Kennedy allowed. "... And I know that this bombing is particularly difficult. But if you look, as you know, at any of these struggles over a period,

Memory *In a park in the shadow of Birmingham's 16th Street Baptist Church, a memorial honoring the girls was unveiled on the 50th anniversary of their deaths.*

across the world, it is a very dangerous effort. So everybody just has to keep their nerve." He would send two emissaries to Birmingham. One of them was the former football coach at West Point.

Given the momentous nature of the times, it is understandable that the significance of the 16th Street bombing was not immediately clear to those struggling with the complexities of the battle against Jim Crow. So much was happening so fast; so much blood was being shed.

Hearing the news of the bombing on the radio, John Lewis, the young activist, traveled to Birmingham from his parents' home in Pike County, Alabama. At dusk on the day of the attack he was there outside the sanctuary, wondering. "It was unreal to stand there and try to absorb what had happened," Lewis recalled. "I looked at the people standing on that sidewalk across the street, these black men and women of Birmingham, who had lived through so much, and I knew that they had to be asking themselves, How much *more*? What *else*? What's *next*? ... Four children killed on a Sunday morning in church, in God's house. What *could* be next?"

It was a question that tragically had an answer: Dallas, and the murder of the president of the United States, which brought Lyndon Johnson to ultimate power. And Johnson, for all his manifold sins, was determined to finish the work of Lincoln by liberating a captive people.

The fact that such liberation was required is an uncomfortable reality at the heart of our history. The mechanics of memory are particularly fraught in the American South, where so much unfolded the day before yesterday. There is a natural human tendency to want to shut the door on a painful past, to push it away, to say *that belonged to another time.* When we're being totally honest with ourselves, however, we know that William Faulkner was right when he observed, in *Requiem for a Nun,* that the past is never dead; it isn't even past. The question for leaders like Bell and cities like Birmingham thus becomes *how,* not *whether,* to deal with a troubled history.

In an act of civic candor entitled "Fifty Years Forward," Birmingham marked the 50th anniversary of 1963 forthrightly, acknowledging the city's sins but understandably asking for the nation—and the world—to see the city in full, not just for what it was then but for what it is now. "My thought all along is be exactly who you are," says Bell. "There's nothing we can do to change our past. We are who we are. What is oftentimes missed with Birmingham is the city we've become. The images are always about the dogs and the hoses. And yes, that's who we were, but we've come out of that. Now is the time to showcase Birmingham for who we are."

Which is a Southern city trying to make its way economically and culturally. The Jackie Robinson movie *42* was filmed in Birmingham, which boasts a new minor-league ballpark for the Southern League's Birmingham Barons. Mercedes and Honda have built plants in Alabama in recent times. Mayor Bell spends his time talking up investments in the University of Alabama at Birmingham's medical research center.

Such things were unimaginable half a century ago. No city played a larger role in the midcentury war over the fate of Jim Crow than Birmingham. In Alabama governor George C. Wallace and in Birmingham public-safety commissioner Eugene "Bull" Connor, civil rights leaders King, Fred Shuttlesworth and others found formidable foes whose violent opposition to the movement vividly dramatized the stakes of the struggle. The images of fire hoses and snarling dogs come from here; the face of Jesus was blown out of one of the 16th Street church's windows during the attack, an eerie and enduring symbol of a world where hate, at least in the moment of the bombing, overshadowed love.

For Mayor Bell—and for Birmingham, and for the country—the movement and its martyrs changed everything. "Their sacrifice made my life possible, made my being the mayor of Birmingham possible," he says. "My biggest hope was a job in the mines or the steel mills. But now opportunities abound because of 1963." Out of terror came hope.

Today a memorial window, a gift from the people of Wales, depicts a crucified Jesus and a quotation from Matthew 25: "Inasmuch as ye have done it unto the least of these my brethren, ye have done it unto me." The Jesus in the window is a black man, arms outstretched, reaching, it seems, to a future beyond the blood and the bombs—a future that is far closer to reality now than appeared even remotely possible when the Klan's bomb ripped through the stone of the church and the flesh of the churchgoers.

Fifty years ago, King preached at the funeral for three of the four victims. "God still has a way of wringing good out of evil," he said. "And history has proven over and over again that unmerited suffering is redemptive. The innocent blood of these little girls may well serve as a redemptive force that will bring new light to this dark city." And so it has.

CHAPTER SEVEN

THE BRIDGE TO FREEDOM

AFTER WINNING THE CIVIL RIGHTS ACT OF 1964, THE
MOVEMENT STALLED IN WASHINGTON UNTIL THE
SPECTACLE OF BLOODY SUNDAY OUTRAGED AMERICA
AND MOVED LBJ TO ACTION

BY LANI GUINIER

CONGRESS DID NOT pass and President Lyndon Johnson did not sign the Civil Rights Act of 1964 and the Voting Rights Act of 1965 simply because it was the right thing to do. Both were pushed by a mass movement to guarantee civil rights for all. The success of that movement, to quote Martin Luther King Jr., depended on ordinary people sending their message with "the blunt pen of marching ranks." Nowhere did these marchers sound clearer than in Selma, Alabama.

Selma is the county seat of Dallas County, the heart of the Black Belt, so called because of its rich soil and the poor people who worked it. The region was one of the capitals of American slavery, and long after the Civil War the area retained its black majority. Nevertheless, in 1964 only a handful of the county's black residents could vote. Whites controlled all 10 county commissions, 11 boards of education and 34 town governments.

Strides *President Lyndon Johnson signs the Civil Rights Bill into law on July 2, 1964, urging all Americans to eliminate injustice.*

Dallas County's political situation resulted from decades of pervasive disenfranchisement. Although the Fifteenth Amendment in 1870 ostensibly extended the franchise to the nation's male black residents, for the next 95 years Alabama's state and local governments restricted black turnout. In 1901, a year after 181,471 black Alabamans voted, white citizens enacted a new state constitution that disenfranchised virtually all black residents. In Dallas County, where 9,871 black residents voted in 1900, only 52 black voters remained in Selma, the county seat — a situation that did not improve through the 1960s. As the Southern Organizing Committee for Economic and Social Justice described the area in the 1960s, "geographically, politically and economically, the Black Belt has been the South's 'South.' "

The Black Belt's white politicians exploited the area's poverty and fear with strict Jim Crow laws. Albert Turner, a resident of nearby Perry County, recalled that "the sheriff was the power. I mean, he was everything. Whatever he said, when you got arrested, that was it." Every judge was white, there were few black lawyers, and black residents were generally not allowed into the courthouse except to pay taxes. This biased legal system was supplemented by violence and intimidation against black residents who sought to vote. Turner continued, "There was not a black registered voter from 1955 to 1965 in Perry County. You just did not register."

CHOOSING THE BATTLEGROUND

In 1964, at the invitation of Dallas County's lone black lawyer, J.L. Chestnut, and encouraged by local organizers, the Atlanta-based Southern Christian Leadership Conference and its president, Martin Luther King Jr., agreed on Selma as the hub for a nationally credible, locally grounded voting-rights campaign. The idea was to have local activists organize daytime and even riskier night vigils outside the local courthouses to focus attention on the way the scales of justice were manipulated directly to exclude blacks. With Dr. King's participation in the protests, the SCLC hoped to assure the attention of journalists, especially if something visually dramatic occurred. The goal was to galvanize the national conscience, provoke federal intervention, and then have people in place to carry forward whatever the federal authorities might initiate. From the SCLC's perspective, only the national government could stop the white Southern terrorists who operated in Alabama with the implicit sanction of both private and public authority.

While young activists like Diane Nash proposed dramatic local agitation to persuade the federal government to act, King believed he could appeal to Washington politicians by talking to them in person. But his visits were fruitless. Despite the worldwide prestige King's receipt of the Nobel Peace Prize generated in December 1964, he arrived back in the U.S. without fanfare when he and and a principal aide, Andrew Young, met with Attorney General Nicholas Katzenbach, Vice President Hubert Humphrey and President Johnson in two unproductive sessions. In his memoir, *An Easy Burden*, Young recounts the meetings: "I'm sure we can't get a voting rights bill, not in 1965," Humphrey pleaded. "We passed the civil rights bill only a few months ago. It's too soon." At the White House, President Johnson spent the entire session talking about what was already in the works. As he left Washington, King realized that Johnson, like Kennedy before him, was not prepared to initiate bold new legislation on his own.

By late December, King decided that he would go to Selma and join forces with the advocates of more dramatic action. The Student Nonviolent Coordinating Committee (SNCC), a group of college students formed in the wake of the first Woolworth's sit-ins in Greensboro, N.C., sent three organizers to work with local ministers including Bernard Lafayette to press for voter registration. John Lewis, then an organizer for SNCC and now a congressman from Atlanta, was soon arrested

Protest *Chaos erupts on the Edmund Pettus Bridge as marchers are assulted by state troopers.*

simply for carrying a "One Man, One Vote" sign outside the Dallas County courthouse. Activists like Lafayette and Lewis were natural political-campaign workers, with unbounded enthusiasm for face-to-face persuasion. They organized "citizenship schools," conducted by people from the community who could read and write, turning every barbershop into a school for filling out a voter-registration application.

Soon after King arrived in Selma, the intemperate Dallas County sheriff, Jim Clark, arrested King and several thousand protestors for parading without a permit and unlawful assembly. While in jail in February 1965, King wrote a letter to the *New York Times*: "This is Selma, Alabama. There are more Negroes in jail with me than there are on the voting rolls." King again met with President Johnson to discuss voting rights legislation soon after he was released from jail. But it was not King's visits to Washington that finally convinced the president to introduce legislation; it was ordinary people doing extraordinary things.

On February 18, Jimmie Lee Jackson, a 27-year-old black pulpwood cutter, was shot by state troopers when he tried to protect his mother from the clubs of troopers breaking up a night vigil. After Jackson died several days later, young activists threatened to carry his body to Montgomery and present it to Governor George Wallace. Local leaders converted the angry sentiments into a plan to walk to Montgomery from Selma to petition Wallace for the right to vote. It was a Sunday when, in full view of TV cameras, these marchers, including organizers Amelia Boynton, John Lewis and Albert Turner, approached the Edmund Pettus Bridge, which had been blocked by Alabama state troopers and white civilian volunteers deputized by Sheriff Clark.

As the marchers approached, the troopers sounded a "two-minute" warning. Then, without waiting more than a few seconds, they attacked. A state trooper's club hit Mrs. Boynton on the

The Right to Vote *King watching LBJ's address to Congress days after Bloody Sunday*

back of the neck and she fell to the ground. While she was regaining consciousness, she heard someone ordering her to get up and run or she would be teargassed. Former U.S. Senator Harris Wofford, who came to Selma to join a subsequent march, describes Mrs. Boynton's eyewitness account of what came to be known as Bloody Sunday: "Then the teargas can was dropped next to her head. To a mounted posse, Sheriff Clark shouted, 'Get those goddamn niggers! Get those goddamn white niggers!' and the horsemen charged with bullwhips. 'Deputies' using the electric cattle prods chased the marchers still on their feet all the way back to Brown's Chapel." Broadcasts of the event resembled a battle scene, with smoke and mass chaos. Widespread public outrage erupted after video clips were shown on national TV, interrupting the ABC Sunday night movie, *Judgment at Nuremberg*.

King missed Bloody Sunday; he had been in Atlanta delivering a sermon. As images of the march galvanized the nation, King's absence led more-militant organizers to challenge his political credibility. These younger activists were determined to follow up the march that had been aborted on Bloody Sunday. In part to reassert his leadership, King agreed to lead a second march the following Tuesday, March 9. The NAACP Legal Defense Fund's lawyers sought an injunction prohibiting Gov. Wallace from interfering with the follow-up procession. But Judge Frank Johnson, a usually sympathetic federal judge based in Montgomery, surprised the LDF by issuing a restraining order prohibiting the march temporarily. That Tuesday, with Judge Johnson's injunction still in effect, King staged a symbolic march, leading 1,500 people to the Edmund Pettus Bridge, where they kneeled in prayer and then turned around. As Jack Greenberg writes in his book on the LDF, *Crusaders in the Courts*, "Martin had hit upon a brilliant solution, for while it puzzled both followers and opponents who had not expected the march to halt in the prayer, it focused world attention on Selma, avoided violence and did not defy [Judge] Johnson's injunction."

PERSUADING THE PRESIDENT

As the country responded with outrage to what they perceived as insufficient federal intervention, President Johnson remained confused and somewhat hostile. "Why are they demonstrating against me?" Johnson demanded when he met the next day in the Cabinet Room with NAACP head Roy Wilkins and other civil rights leaders. "I've passed all these civil rights bills. I've made speeches." Late that same week, the president called a meeting of the Council on Civil Rights, chaired by Humphrey and attended by Secretary of Labor Willard Wirtz and many other officials. Seated at the head of a big table in the Indian Treaty Room, Humphrey spoke of his concern that the demonstrations in Selma might be the work of outside agitators or communists. He then asked the table for their candid advice. Secretary of Labor Wirtz was the first to speak, calling for an immediate voting rights bill. But Wirtz was one of the few men in the room who did so. Also attending was Roger Wilkins, Roy's nephew, of the Department of Commerce. When it was his turn, Wilkins's voice rang out loud and clear: "Mr. Vice President, I agree with Secretary Wirtz. The president needs to send up a voting rights bill to Congress ... We don't need a perfect bill. We need a bill. Congress will change the bill anyway. The president should say this bill is necessary for democracy. He should say this in the most forceful way possible. I am disappointed, Mr. Vice President, that you see this as the work of outside agitators. These are American citizens demanding American rights ... This is the central cause of justice — to enlarge our democracy."

Wilkins's outburst changed the tone of the meeting. It probably also forestalled any more waffling by the White House. Two days later, the president went to the Rose Garden and declared that the time for action was at hand. He immediately proceeded to introduce the voting legislation that King and Young had pleaded for privately, announcing his plan of action to a joint session of Congress. He placed Selma alongside Lexington and Concord and Appomattox as turning points where "history and fate meet at a single time in a single place" to shape our "unending search for freedom." Speaking "as a man whose roots go deeply into Southern soil," Johnson said to a hushed chamber: "There is no Negro problem. There is no Southern problem. There is no Northern problem. There is only an American problem." Johnson told Congress that "the real hero of this struggle is the American Negro." "Their cause must be our cause too. Because it is not just Negroes, but really all of us who must overcome the crippling legacy of bigotry and injustice. And we shall overcome!" King, inspired by the soaring rhetoric and decisive action, dutifully waited until Judge Johnson lifted the injunction to command a full-scale march to Montgomery, protected this time by Alabama National Guard troops who answered to federal authority.

On August 6, Johnson signed the Voting Rights Act of 1965, providing for registration by federal examiners in any state or county where fewer than half of the adults were registered to vote. The civil rights movement gained the national legislation it needed when it found leadership within a broad-based coalition of heroic hearts and joined those people in motion. By speaking words with their feet, ordinary black people found a way to tell their stories so that all of America could understand.

Lani Guinier is a professor at Harvard Law School, formerly with the NAACP Legal Defense Fund, and author of Lift Every Voice: Turning a Civil Rights Setback into a New Vision of Social Justice.

Light the Way *Two years after the Stonewall riots, taking to the streets of New York City for a candlelight parade during Gay Liberation Week*

IN HIS STEPS

KING'S BELIEF IN NONVIOLENCE WAS
GALVANIZING, BUT THE CIVIL RIGHTS
MOVEMENTS THAT FOLLOWED HAD TO
FIND THEIR OWN WAYS TO EXPRESS IT

BY JOHN CLOUD

TORNADOES THREATENED TENNESSEE the night before Martin

Luther King Jr. was murdered. At least seven people would die just across the Mississippi River in Arkansas, and King's family wanted him home—which, for the time being, was the Lorraine Motel in Memphis.

But as writer Taylor Branch points out in *At Canaan's Edge: America in the King Years 1965-68*, King felt almost incandescent pressure to show up at Mason Temple, a Pentecostal church where at least a thousand people were assembling to hear him speak at the height of what had become a national controversy over the basic rights and pay of Memphis sanitation workers. Around 9:30 on April 3, 1968, after much debate among his staff, King finally did take the microphone at Mason. The room shuddered at his arrival. As Branch retells it, King grew expansive in his remarks. "If I were standing at the beginning of time," he said—and could choose any lifetime— he would consider the glories of ancient Greece, Egypt and Rome. "But I wouldn't stop there. If you could allow me to live just a few years in the second half of the 20th century, I will be happy." Branch explains: "It might seem strange with the world so messed up, King said, but he chose above all to see the stirrings of a human-rights revolution for freedom worldwide."

But did that vision achieve lasting valence? King's years of exuberance inspired millions, but it's fair to ask how his ideas for civil rights applied broadly to other minorities and oppressed citizens—whether his capacity to rouse dazzling outrage lasted beyond what befell him at the Lorraine. Women, immigrants, gays, the impoverished—many who could have seen their aspirations for U.S. equality amplified after King—found themselves in a familiar place in the aftermath of his death: one in which they had barely moved. Yet 50 years later, King would barely recognize the America he helped create. While his central tenet of nonviolence was galvanizing in the moment, the way in which it influenced the civil rights movements that followed was both subtle and gradual, a revolution half a century in the making.

THE IDEAS OF GANDHI

The political movement for women's equality both predated the racial civil rights movement and, in some ways, outshone it. It took until the early 20th century for American women to gain the right to vote. In 1920, with mostly Republican support, the Senate ratified the 19th Amendment, which finally enfranchised women. It was a glorious victory, but scores of municipal laws and cultural mores kept women from anything like full equality until well after the King era.

King was a minor figure in women's rights. In her definitive 1995 biography *The Education of a Woman: The Life of Gloria Steinem*, feminist author Carolyn Heilbrun mentions King in passing just three times in 450 pages. King had never won the respect of many feminists partly because of his relentless philandering (as Branch writes, King kept a stable of "regular mistresses"). King's lodestar was the idea of nonviolence; he had more trouble with the idea of fidelity.

Regardless, the movement for women's rights, particularly on a global scale, proceeded apace during the 1970s and '80s with implicit, sometimes controversial, deference to two great principles of nonviolence that King had espoused at every turn: *satyagraha* and *ahimsa*. King had borrowed both ideas from Gandhi. The first, *satyagraha*, is the notion of passive resistance—insisting that injustice be recognized as truth. *Ahimsa* is simpler: the concept of not injuring others.

Staying true to nonviolent principles has been most difficult in the abortion fight. Since the 1973 Roe v. Wade decision, anti-abortion activists have murdered at least eight people

Forward March *On New York's Fifth Avenue 50 years after the passage of the 19th Amendment*

who worked at abortion clinics. But for the women's movement, the impulse toward revenge led to the courts. "You have to remember, the National Organization for Women was, in part, inspired by the civil rights movement," says Terry O'Neill, 61, the president of NOW. "We have responded in the streets with protests to try to get laws changed." On the abortion front, a chief nonviolent response has been to seek legislation preventing people from approaching women entering abortion clinics. Conservatives have argued that such laws violate the First Amendment, and the Supreme Court announced in 2013 that it will review a Massachusetts law that restricts protests near abortion-providing facilities. O'Neill says the laws are a necessity for women who seek not just nonviolence but what she calls non-engagement: "The principle is that even when people are saying nasty, mean things to these women—sometimes women just seeking prenatal care—we verbally don't engage. And let me tell you, it can be personally very, very difficult to maintain that stance of non-engagement." But O'Neill says non-engagement can be just as powerful as nonviolence—which is, in short, a way of defusing the power of any given confrontation.

UPRISING AT THE STONEWALL INN

In the '60s, militant leftists in the U.S. had a great problem embracing concepts of nonviolence, not least because the police and especially J. Edgar Hoover's FBI deployed violence whenever they saw fit. During the 1970s, female activists continued to hew to *satyagraha* and *ahimsa* (a few burned bras and women's-only music festivals probably don't count as violations), but one of

Stand Strong *Coretta Scott King joins Cesar Chavez in a 1973 boycott in New York City.*

the most important movements to flourish in the wake of King's ascendance started explicitly with violence—violence that is honored every year in parades across the world.

It was around 1:20 a.m. on June 28, 1969, a little more than a year after King was shot in Memphis, when eight policemen stomped into the Stonewall Inn, a dive in Manhattan's Greenwich Village that had no liquor license but served watery cocktails to a mix of drag queens, street kids, gay professionals, and closeted and straight mafiosi (who ran the place). Within two hours, the Village was bleeding and burning as hundreds rioted. How did the nightly saturnalia at Stonewall produce protests that would kick-start the modern gay-rights movement? The uprising was inspirited by a potent cocktail of pent-up rage (raids of gay bars were brutal and routine), over-wrought emotions (hours earlier, thousands had wept at the funeral of Judy Garland) and drugs.

As a 17-year-old cross-dresser was being led into a paddy wagon and got a shove from a cop, she fought back. "[She] hit the cop and was so stoned, she didn't know what she was doing—or didn't care," one of her friends later told Martin Duberman, author of the history *Stonewall*.

Later, the deputy police inspector in charge would explain that day's impact: "For those of us in [the] public morals [division], things were completely changed ... Suddenly they were not submissive anymore." Today gays and lesbians memorialize that night each year with a weekend of rallies, parades and parties. In 2013, the celebration was all the more intense since the Supreme Court had just invalidated key parts of the so-called Defense of Marriage Act, which had prohibited any federal recognition of gay couples.

Yet commemorating the riots seems at odds with King's principles of nonviolence. Both police officers and gay people had their faces bloodied with glass and fists; bottles and bricks rained down on Grove Street and Seventh Avenue South. Still, no one died. And gay historians point out that for the most part, gays have benefited from and lived up to King's principles. "You have to remember, that was the summer of 1969, at the tail end of years when many cities were convulsed by violence," says George Chauncey, a Yale professor of American history. "[Stonewall] was an incredibly nonviolent protest when you compare it to Detroit or Newark just a few years earlier."

Similarly, activists such as Cesar Chavez had been demonstrating how nonviolence could work—to a point—as he advocated for the rights of farmworkers in California. In 1965, a group of mostly Filipino workers in the breadbasket town of Delano, Calif., quit working because, among other reasons, they were not earning the federal minimum wage, $1.25. Within a few days, Chavez joined their strike, which was a mixed success. Growers ensured that grapes continued to be harvested even as the farmworkers and Chavez spent years agonizing for higher pay and arguing the benefits of nonviolence. Chavez underwent a 25-day hunger strike that took a great toll on his health. But Chavez did use one tactic that, while technically nonviolent, won him great respect. He sent a team to follow one of the picketed growers from Delano to the Oakland docks, where the grapes were going to be shipped. Chavez's three-member team, including a student, persuaded the longshoremen not to load the shipment of grapes, so that 10,000 tons of grapes rotted. In 1969, grape growers signed their first union contract.

A MAN OF CONTRADICTIONS

King himself had trouble understanding how to make nonviolence the center of a rights movement. Some of the reasons were personal. Hoover, who judged King a naive proto-Communist, had his soldiers hound King until the day he died. King's phones were tapped; his mistresses were followed; his mail was opened. He was creating a civil rights movement even as his own civil liberties had become largely notional. The contradictions multiplied: King's income was paid at least partly by the Ford Foundation, which meant he had to answer to a large board of American grandees, even as he was surrounded by activists who wanted to tear down the old system.

Also, a central question hovered around King's main effort: Why was he advocating for nonviolence in a violent world? How could civil rights movements proceed against governments so unethical as those run by Lyndon Johnson and, later, Richard Nixon? "Why are you teaching nonviolence to Negroes in Mississippi but not to Lyndon Johnson?" asked James Bevel, a colleague of King's. Simultaneously, Johnson aides pushed against King from the other side. White House adviser John Roche told the president in a private communiqué that King "has thrown in with the commies." Thinking about how King's agenda would be perceived in the future, Roche wrote to Johnson that King was "painting himself into a corner with a bunch of losers," presumably the union men in Memphis or farmworkers in California, though Roche didn't make himself clear.

Whatever the case, King would die in a world of contradictions, many of them of his own making. His poor treatment of women; his indifference to gay colleagues suffering in the closet; his overpowering religiosity; his total embrace of nonviolence—these contradictions would rightly be played out in the struggles that followed him, particularly after 9/11 further complicated our notions of how to respond to violence. King defined the best way to approach enemies—with as much love as you can muster—and he once commented that all social movements run on "tempered lunacy." It was perfect King: a joke, a sermon, and a reality all in one.

CHAPTER NINE

AFTER TRAYVON

**THE FLORIDA TEEN'S DEATH RENEWED
OUTRAGE OVER THE PLIGHT OF AMERICA'S
YOUNG BLACK MEN**

BY MICHAEL SCHERER AND ELIZABETH DIAS

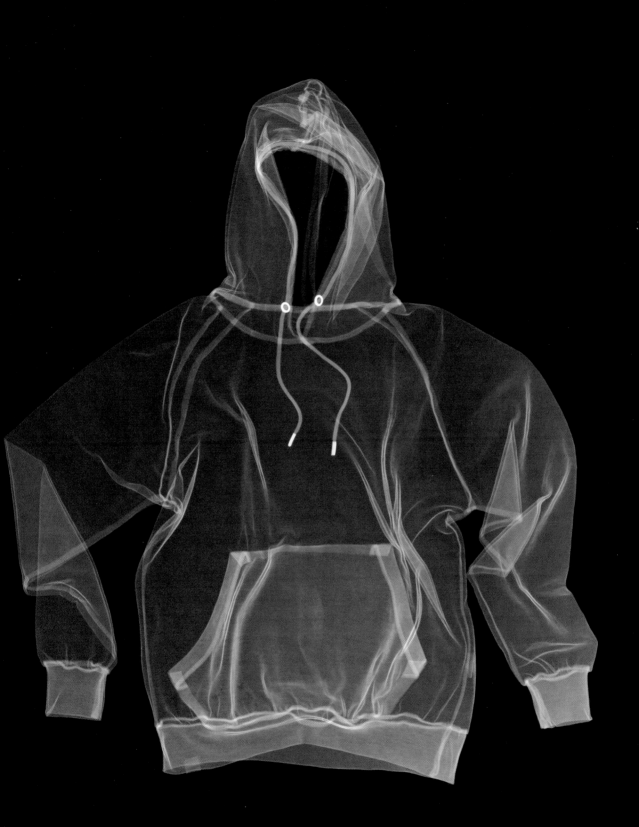

SHORTLY AFTER DAWN most Sundays, a dozen or so black pastors gather by

conference call to pray and compare notes for their sermons later that morning. But on July 14, 2013, when Howard-John Wesley called in at 6 a.m., there were already more than 100 pastors on the line, and his computer showed 57 tweets from members of his congregation, Alfred Street Baptist in Alexandria, Va., all with the same questions: What would he say to help heal the hurt and anger after the verdict the night before? How would he deal with the fact that a neighborhood watchman, George Zimmerman, had been found not guilty after shooting dead an unarmed black 17-year-old named Trayvon Martin?

Many of the preachers had families of their own, and the case had made them think about their children's safety. Nathan Scovens, who leads Galilee Missionary Baptist in Winston-Salem, N.C., said his son had asked him, "Daddy, is George Zimmerman going to heaven?" Otis Moss III, the pastor of Barack Obama's old Chicago church, Trinity United Church of Christ, said that after the verdict his 12-year-old asked simply, "Daddy, am I next?"

Hours later, when the pews had filled, the message was clear. America has been facing challenges like the Martin slaying for generations. Every few years, some instance of probable profiling, police overreaction or malice grabs national attention. A young black man dies or is brutally injured. The resulting investigation and trial become national dramas, driven less by the case file than by the state of race in America, the pent-up furies that seethe beneath the national narrative of progress. The names are written in history: Emmett Till, Yusuf Hawkins, Rodney King, Amadou Diallo and now Trayvon Martin. Presidents comment; protesters fill the streets and, more recently, send tweets. And then it all seems to go away.

For the black pastors who preached that Sunday, their messages were filled with familiar outrage over injustice. But they also embedded in their sermons a determination that this time be different, that the Martin death not be seen in isolation and the controversy not fade from public view. Just weeks earlier, the Supreme Court had voided a key part of the Voting Rights Act protecting minorities in states with a history of discrimination. A celebrity chef's empire had imploded when she admitted to using racial epithets. Over the long Fourth of July holiday, 72 people were shot in Chicago, many of them young black men. The 50th anniversary of Martin Luther King Jr.'s March on Washington loomed around the corner. "Paula Deen, a Supreme Court decision, and now this," Wesley preached the day after the Zimmerman verdict. "There's a racial consciousness that rises up within me that somehow takes my ability to see this objectively. I am angry."

The outrage was not limited to churches. In largely peaceful protests across the country, organizers tried to channel campaigns against gun violence, police profiling and "stand your ground" laws, a relatively new legal trend that expands protections for citizens who kill strangers when threatened. In North Carolina, a growing weekly protest against Republican-enacted social policies organized largely by black clergy, called Moral Monday, swelled to vent the anger over the verdict. Addressing the National Association for the Advancement of Colored People in Florida, U.S. Attorney General Eric Holder recalled the time a cop stopped him on his way to a movie in a predominantly white Washington neighborhood. He was a federal prosecutor at the time. Holder, too, had talked with his children about profiling, just as his father had spoken to him. "That is a father-son tradition I hoped would not need to be handed down," he told the crowd.

Among black leaders, the hope is to defeat the national instinct to move on until the next

THE TALK
HOW PARENTS RAISING BLACK BOYS TRY TO KEEP THEIR SONS SAFE

BY JEANNINE AMBER

Certain events have a way of changing everything, reorganizing life into an unforgettable before and after. For New Orleans residents, it was the hour the levees broke and their city began to flood; for New Yorkers, it was the terror of Sept. 11, 2001. Before, there is an order to things. After, there is a danger that feels imminent, unpredictable and wild.

For black parents, the new demarcation between before and after was the moment we watched George Zimmerman walk free after being tried in the shooting death of Trayvon Martin. Before the jury announced its not-guilty verdict, black parents understood what we were up against as we sought to protect our sons. We knew our boys, adored and full of promise, might be treated like criminals by police even though they had committed no crimes. We were painfully reminded of this danger by the deaths of other people's sons, like Sean Bell, who was shot and killed on the morning of his wedding in 2006 by New York City police who incorrectly thought there was a gun in his car; or Oscar Grant III, who was fatally shot in 2009 by a transit cop in Oakland, Calif., while restrained and facedown; or unarmed college student Kendrec McDade, who was killed in 2012 when San Francisco police saw him clutching his waistband and assumed he had a firearm. To gird against the danger that could result from our boys' being profiled, we gave our sons the Talk.

At kitchen tables, during drives to school and in parting words as we sent them off to college, we shared a version of the same lessons given to young black men for generations: "If you are stopped by a cop, do what he says, even if he's harassing you, even if you didn't do anything wrong. Let him arrest you, memorize his badge number, and call me as soon as you get to the precinct. Keep your hands where he can see them. Do not reach for your wallet. Do not grab your phone. Do not raise your voice. Do not talk back. Do you understand me?" Parents in communities besieged by gun violence might add a coda, admonishing their sons to come home right after school, close the blinds, stay inside.

These warnings weren't always heeded, and sometimes they weren't enough. But they allowed parents to feel that we gave our children a measure of protection against a threat we could identify. When confronted by violent gangs or overzealous law enforcement, we knew these rules of engagement might help keep our sons safe. But in George Zimmerman we saw a new danger, one that seemed utterly lawless.

We may never know exactly what happened the night Zimmerman shot Trayvon, but black parents know this: a neighborhood watchman saw a brown-skinned teenager—a boy who could have been one of ours—wearing a hoodie pulled up against the rain and assumed he was up to no good. That suspicion set into motion a chain of events that left the boy dead. How do we protect against that? Do we tell our children to run if they are being followed? Or should they stop and turn around? Do we tell them to defend themselves, as Trayvon appears to have done, or to get on the ground like Oscar Grant?

Police are trained to ascertain risk, yet studies have shown that they are likely to shoot at an African American suspect faster than at a white one. What about the untrained civilian? Armed with bias and a handgun, how likely is he to see a threat where none exists?

Before Trayvon, we had the Talk to guard our children against danger. After Zimmerman's acquittal in his death, we realize with anguish that there may be little we can do to protect them.

Jeannine Amber is the senior writer at Essence.

Taking a Stand *Protestors march in the streets around New York City's Union Square following George Zimmerman's acquittal.*

racially charged crossroads. "It is time to dust off the formula that worked for our forefathers and foremothers in the civil rights movement," Wesley said days after his sermon. "Pray, march and demand change from every corner of your government."

RACE, NARRATIVES AND REALITY

But for that to happen, there will need to be a new national discussion about how America handles its diversity. The past five years have featured two contradictory narratives. The first is about Obama and the emerging coalition of young and minority voters who elected him twice. In the 2012 election, the percentage of turnout among blacks exceeded that of whites for the first time in history; by roughly 2045, whites will no longer be the majority of the population. Within a year, a majority of children under the age of 5 will be from minority groups. This is the story of promise for much of the country, a signal that the nation can move beyond its tainted past, and it has coincided with a clear rise in optimism among African Americans. A year after Obama's first election as president, 53% of blacks in a survey by the Pew Research Center said that the future for blacks would be better, compared with 44% of those asked the same question in 2007.

But the promise of tomorrow, it turns out, has changed little in the present. Obama's election coincided with a national economic collapse that has hammered minority communities far harder than white ones. From 2007 to 2010, according to the Urban Institute, black family wealth fell by 31%, compared with an 11% decline for whites. For blacks, the national unemployment epidemic was simply more virulent, with the 13.7% black unemployment rate more than twice the 6.6% rate of whites. "Forty percent of our children are growing up in poverty," says Eddie Glaude Jr., who chairs the Center for African American Studies at Princeton University. "We're experiencing what I would call a black Great Depression."

The historic decrease in crime over the past two decades has also not changed the fact that black communities remain the most vulnerable, as both the targets of criminals and

Come Together *Thousands marched, some with signs that read "We are all Trayvon Martin."*

of police enforcing minor crimes like marijuana possession. Blacks make up 13% of the nation's population, but more than half of America's homicide victims and culprits were black in 2011. Of the 2.3 million people incarcerated in this country, 1 million are black. "There's no question that African Americans, and particularly African American men, are the most incarcerated group in the history of the world," says Paul Butler, a professor at Georgetown University Law Center.

Racial profiling, the practice of drawing suspicion from skin color, is publicly disavowed but remains widely practiced. A Gallup poll in July 2013 found that more than one quarter of black men ages 18 to 34 say police have treated them unfairly in the previous 30 days. In New York City, a program called stop-and-frisk, which Mayor Michael Bloomberg credited with major crime reductions, allowed police to temporarily detain and search 685,724 people in 2011 without clear evidence of a crime. In a city that is 44% white, more than 90% of those stopped were minorities. "We are in the face of progression and regression simultaneously," says Moss, the pastor of Trinity in Chicago. "We have the progression of people in elected office and the regression of the war on drugs."

MOBILIZING THE OUTRAGE

As the celebration over the emerging America has faded, the frustrating realities have returned to center stage. Gallup reported in 2008 that 70% of Americans believed race relations would improve with Obama's election, but only a third now believe that Obama's victory fulfilled that promise. The president, meanwhile, has so far proved too divisive a public figure to oversee a national conversation on race, despite occasional efforts in his first term. After criticizing the 2009 arrest of Harvard professor Henry Louis Gates Jr. at his home in a misunderstanding with police, Obama was forced to backtrack from saying the officers "acted stupidly." After the Zimmerman trial, the president's only statement—asking the nation to respect the jury's decision—was released by e-mail.

Behind the scenes, often in unnoticed legal proceedings, Obama's Justice Department has tried to sharpen the focus on policing practices and racially motivated crime. There were 141 federal hate-crime convictions in Obama's first term, up 74% from the previous four years. The department's civil rights division has opened 15 policing investigations, issued eight warning letters after finding misconduct, and negotiated 10 agreements to reform, up from eight investigations and no warning letters or reform agreements in George W. Bush's second term.

But such numbers are of little consolation given the perceived scale of the problem in black communities. More likely to have an impact in this era of viral, do-it-yourself media is Nikkolas Smith, a Los Angeles artist whose Photoshopped image of Martin Luther King Jr. wearing a hoodie like Trayvon's exploded on social media after the verdict. He called the piece *April 4, 1968: Suspect or Saint?* "It's amazing the fearful reaction some people have when they see the exact same MLK picture they've seen a hundred times, only with a hoodie replacing the suit and tie," Smith told TIME. Notes Robin D.G. Kelley, a professor of American history at the University of California, Los Angeles, "What makes this different is the sheer number of people who are outraged and are mobilizing seems to be greater, and it is greater because of social media."

RETURN OF THE PASTORS?

The Rev. Calvin Butts III, pastor of Abyssinian Baptist Church in Harlem, was in Chicago when the jury delivered the verdict, and he knew he had to send a strong message to his congregation. "We are not in a postracial society," he said later. "Now, as far as I am concerned, is the time for pushback. I mean serious pushback."

Bishop Eric Freeman, pastor of the Meeting Place, a 500-member church outside Columbia, S.C., decided to add a clinic called Live 2 Tell to its annual back-to-school program, to teach young African American men how to minimize themselves as racial-profiling targets and how to respond when they are profiled. "We have to have a four-pronged approach," says the Rev. William Barber II, who organized the Moral Monday protests in Raleigh. "We've got to protect voting rights, because voting rights is the way we get many of the people on our court systems. Two, we've got to repeal 'stand your ground.' Three, we've got to pass anti-racial-profiling laws. Four, we have to stand against violence and the proliferation of guns."

The Justice Department will investigate possible civil rights charges against Zimmerman, a process that could take months and that experts say is unlikely to lead anywhere, since the criminal trial revealed no clear evidence that he was motivated by race. But that didn't stop churches from organizing protests, including a vigil on July 20, 2013, in Washington and other cities.

The immediate policy changes, like the trial itself, may do little to satisfy a country at the intersection of demographic change that promises a new chapter and ancient divisions that refuse to heal. Terry Alexander, a preacher and South Carolina state representative, says he sees in Martin's death a clear metaphor for the changes the nation must undertake. "We're so afraid of losing what we have, or what we own, that we would kill each other even if we have the slightest inclination that you might take something from me. And that's a bad attitude," he says. "The norm is the browning of America, and that's what we need to be moving toward. And there's enough for everybody."

—WITH REPORTING BY MASSIMO CALABRESI, MILES GRAHAM AND MAYA RHODAN/WASHINGTON; CHRISTOPHER MATTHEWS, NATE RAWLINGS AND ANDREA SACHS/NEW YORK

THE ZIMMERMAN MIND-SET
WHY BLACK MEN ARE THE PERMANENT UNDERCASTE

BY MICHELLE ALEXANDER

Back in 1903, in his groundbreaking book *The Souls of Black Folk*, W.E.B. Du Bois argued that the defining element of African American life was being viewed as a perpetual problem—one's very existence as a problem to be dealt with, managed and controlled but never solved. More than 100 years later, Du Bois's rhetorical question seems as relevant as ever: How does it feel to be a problem?

There is a profound difference, of course, between having problems—which all people are allowed—and being a problem. One of the reasons Trayvon Martin's tragic death resonated so powerfully with millions of people of color, black and brown men in particular, is that it was one of those rare situations in this so-called era of colorblindness when suddenly the curtain was pulled back. All the usual rationalizations for routinely treating young black men as problems and up to no good were stripped away. There was just a teenager on the phone with a girl, carrying a bag of Skittles and an iced tea, and he was viewed for no logical reason as scary, out of place, on drugs—someone who needed to be confronted, interrogated and put in place.

Our criminal-justice system has for decades been infected with a mind-set that views black boys and men as a problem. This mind-set has fueled a brutal war on drugs, a get-tough movement and a prison-building boom unprecedented in world history.

Today, millions of people of color are stopped, interrogated and frisked as they are walking to school, driving to church or heading home from the store. In 2011 alone, the New York City police department stopped and frisked more than 600,000 people. The overwhelming majority were black and brown men who were innocent of any crime or infraction. Their mere existence was cause for concern, just as the sight of Trayvon Martin walking leisurely through his own neighborhood was enough to make George Zimmerman call the police.

Studies have consistently shown that people of color are no more likely to use or sell illegal drugs than whites, yet black people have been arrested and incarcerated at grossly disproportionate rates during the 40-year-old war on drugs. If people who abuse illegal drugs were viewed as people who have real problems—rather than people who are problems—then drug treatment would be the obvious and rational response, rather than putting people struggling with addiction in cages, treating them like animals and stamping them with a lifelong badge of inferiority.

Once released from prison, most people find that their punishment is far from over. Felons are typically stripped of the very rights supposedly won in the civil rights movement, including the right to vote, the right to serve on juries, and the right to be free of legal discrimination in employment, housing, access to education and public benefits. They're relegated to a permanent undercaste. Unable to find work or housing, most wind up back in prison within a few years. Black men with criminal records are the most severely disadvantaged group in the labor market. In some places, more than 50% of people are in this demographic.

Research shows that racial disparities in violent crime disappear when you control for joblessness. Unemployed men of all races are equally likely to be violent, particularly if they are chronically without work. But rather than viewing high levels of violent crime in ghettoized communities as a symptom of deeper economic and social ills, black men and boys are viewed as the problem itself and treated accordingly. Jobs are promised but almost never delivered, and schools are allowed to fail, as ever bigger prisons are built to manage "the problem."

Trayvon Martin will not be the last black boy who dies or goes to jail or gives up on his life because he was viewed and treated as nothing but a problem. We are all guilty of being too quiet for too long. Let it be said hereafter that we were quiet no more.

Michelle Alexander is a civil rights lawyer and the author of The New Jim Crow: Mass Incarceration in the Age of Colorblindness.

CHAPTER TEN

THE NEW HEROES OF CIVIL RIGHTS

BY CHARLAYNE HUNTER-GAULT, TROY PATTERSON, CYNTHIA TUCKER AND JOSE ANTONIO VARGAS

This decade marks the 50th anniversary of some of the most pivotal moments in the civil rights movement. Five decades after those painful events, the fight continues in new and subtle ways. In this chapter, which originally appeared in *Southern Living*, a sister publication of TIME whose hometown is Birmingham, Ala., the magazine marked the anniversary by selecting four honorees who represent the groups and individuals breaking down the barriers that inhibit liberty, opportunity and dignity for all people. Chosen with the help of a panel of distinguished jurors—Carlotta LaNier, Diane McWhorter, Dr. Lawrence J. Pijeaux Jr., Dr. William Pretzer and Beverly Robertson—*Southern Living*'s New Heroes of Civil Rights personify the next generation of leaders forging a better future without forsaking a bitter past. Go to southernliving.com/heroes to see and hear more about their work.

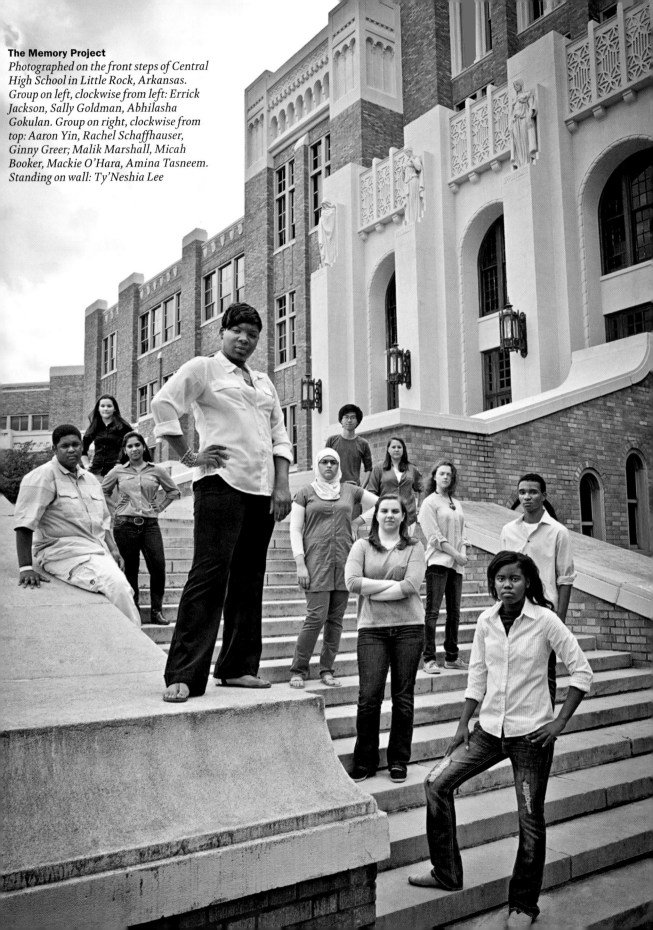

The Memory Project
Photographed on the front steps of Central High School in Little Rock, Arkansas. Group on left, clockwise from left: Errick Jackson, Sally Goldman, Abhilasha Gokulan. Group on right, clockwise from top: Aaron Yin, Rachel Schaffhauser, Ginny Greer; Malik Marshall, Micah Booker, Mackie O'Hara, Amina Tasneem. Standing on wall: Ty'Neshia Lee

STUDENTS OF LITTLE ROCK CENTRAL HIGH

For protecting the future by understanding the past

In 2005, two years before the 50th anniversary of the desegregation of Central High School in Little Rock, Ark., civics teachers George West, Keith Richardson, Cynthia Nunnley and Mike Johnson gave their students an assignment. They wanted them to understand, in a personal way, what took place in their school decades before they were born. They asked the students to interview a relative who lived through the turbulent civil rights years, including the 1957 desegregation of Central High. That semester, history came to life in a way it never could in a history book. In living rooms, across kitchen tables, on front porches at sunset, this generation's students of Central High unlocked doors to powerful memories. The essays they wrote—500 in the first two years—were the start of an ongoing educational experiment: the Memory Project.

Now in its ninth year, the project has captured the imagination of more than 1,500 students and evolved in relevant ways. Initially published on a website—lrchmemory .org—the first oral histories were harvested and published in a book, *Beyond Central, Toward Acceptance*, in 2010. This book became an important tool for the National Park Service (NPS), which hosts 125,000 annual visitors who come to the Little Rock Central High School National Historic Site. *Beyond Central* answers the most frequent visitor questions: Do today's students know about the history of their school? What do they think about civil rights today?

"Although park rangers do lead guided tours into Central on school days, our agreement is that we will not disrupt classes," says NPS ranger Jodi Morris. "Visitors have seldom been able to speak directly to students. The Memory Project's website and publications provide that student/visitor connection."

In 2012, a dozen Central High School volunteers, ages 14 to 18, began archiving a new round of oral histories from other students. They blind-reviewed 300 and chose 45 for a second book, *Mapping the Road to Change: Insights on Perceptions, Prejudice, and Acceptance*.

This book looks at race and beyond for the roots of issues both local and global. Students wrote about anti-Semitism in Cleveland, conflicts between Muslims and Sikhs, and the human-rights protests in Tiananmen Square. They contemplated World War II Japanese internment in U.S. camps as well as discrimination based on sexual orientation and physical disability.

The process presented startling revelations about "things you wouldn't find in a textbook," says student editor Abhilasha Gokulan. "The project starts a conversation among young kids that they would never have had."

Among those interviewed was Thelma Mothershed Wair, a member of the Little Rock Nine. Now in her early 70s, Wair told her teenage grandniece, Amaree Austin, about braving the violent mobs that hurled threats and racial slurs at her and eight other teenagers as they enrolled as the first black students at Central High.

Austin said many of today's students feel far removed from the legacy of the Little Rock Nine. Their attitude, she said, is, "That happened a long time ago."

But the more she listened to her great-aunt, the more she appreciated their courage and determination to be treated as equals—and the more she felt determined to claim it.

"I wanted to share [that history] with others so we can understand where we came from," she said, "to keep us from going back."

By Charlayne Hunter-Gault, an Emmy Award–winning journalist and the author of the young-adult book To the Mountaintop: My Journey Through the Civil Rights Movement

SUSAN GLISSON

For pioneering a community-based model of truth-telling and reconciliation

Through the tumult of the civil rights movement, Mississippi acquired a reputation as the nation's least progressive state—violent, brutal, racist. Dr. Susan Glisson doesn't shy away from that painful past. Instead, she looks that history squarely in the eye and insists that others do the same.

"I believe the truth is the foundation for the future," she says. "Truth-telling [underscores] the whole approach for what we do."

As executive director of the University of Mississippi's William Winter Institute for Racial Reconciliation, Glisson, 46, has spent years bringing together black, white and brown Mississippians, the powerful and the powerless, the descendants of Ku Klux Klan members with descendants of their victims. Her efforts have helped make Mississippi a leader in healing old wounds.

Glisson joined the crusade for justice in one of the state's most notorious cases: the 1964 murders of civil rights workers Andrew Goodman, James Chaney and Michael Schwerner. When Edgar Ray Killen was convicted of three counts of manslaughter in 2005—41 years after the crime—"a gear shifted in Mississippi's universe," Glisson says. The trial inspired her to coordinate the Mississippi Truth Project, a grassroots movement pressing for a commission to investigate racially motivated crimes of the civil rights era. If it is convened, Mississippi would be only the second state, after North Carolina, to undertake such a commission.

Glisson spearheaded a successful effort to pass the nation's first state law that requires the teaching of civil-rights and human-rights history in Mississippi public schools. In 2002 she helped the University of Mississippi organize events to mark the 40th anniversary of the entry of its first black student, James Meredith, whose enrollment sparked deadly riots. The ceremonies included a formal apology from then-chancellor Robert Khayat. No university has done more to acknowledge its role in perpetuating segregation.

Glisson says her mission is social justice—working to change the conditions that have created a legacy of inequities. And she believes that racism can be eliminated in her lifetime. "I don't think it's easy," she says. "It takes hard work. But it can happen. I'm seeing it happen in Mississippi every day."

By Cynthia Tucker, a Pulitzer Prize–winning syndicated columnist and visiting professor at the University of Georgia's Grady College

CRISTINA TZINTZÚN

For supporting the safety and dignity of Texas's undocumented workers

The daughter of a Mexican immigrant and the granddaughter of a Bracero (so named for a guest-worker program in the U.S. from 1942 to 1964), Cristina Tzintzún, 32, is an American citizen who sees immigrants' rights as an issue close to home: her younger stepsister is one of the nation's estimated 11 million undocumented immigrants. As a result, she is a voice and a force addressing a civil rights issue that's particularly relevant to the South today.

"The truth is, Texas and other states heavily rely on undocumented labor," says Tzintzún. The Lone Star State, where she moved a decade ago, is home to the second-largest undocumented population in the country, second to California. Many take construction jobs, and in a state that accounted for 16% of construction permits in the U.S. in 2011 (more than Florida and California combined), this workforce is desperately needed. Still, half of the state's nearly one million construction workers have no papers.

Susan Glisson *Photographed at the University of Mississippi campus in Oxford*

Fighting for compassion and awareness, Tzintzún leads the Austin, Texas–based Workers Defense Project (WDP), one of the best-established worker centers in the South. Founded in 2002, WDP is a non-profit organization devoted to improving the working conditions of low-income and undocumented workers.

Through education and advocacy, Tzintzún, who is also a member of FuturoFund, an Austin-based philanthropic group that serves the Latino community, seeks to protect these workers. In addition to offering basic classes (English, computer literacy, leadership development), Tzintzún and the WDP are helping laborers fight for their paychecks (one in four undocumented workers experiences wage theft) and informing them about their right to safe conditions in the workplace. According to the WDP–University of Texas study "Building Austin, Building Injustice," Texas is ranked the most deadly place to work in construction in the country.

Thanks to these largely unsung efforts, Tzintzún is one of the necessary heroines of the New South. "We need to protect the hardworking immigrants who are helping build our country," she says. "It's a matter of dignity for all workers."

By Jose Antonio Vargas, a Pulitzer Prize–winning journalist, the founder of DefineAmerican.com, and the writer and director of Documented, *a personal documentary on immigration*

JEFFERSON PINDER
For socially conscious art that's accessible, provocative and relevant
Some performance artists just create head-scratching riddles, but Jefferson Pinder gets beneath viewers' skin and opens minds. His most powerful videos and mixed-media pieces explore with visceral immediacy the genre's power to address race and identity.

The 43-year-old Washington, D.C., native is currently putting together one of his most rousing pieces yet. Commissioned by

the Birmingham Museum of Art, *Belly of the Beast* is inspired by the 16th Street Baptist Church bombing that killed four girls 50 years ago. "I was trying to figure out how to create a piece relevant to the bombing," Pinder says.

The site-specific piece gathers his career-defining interests and draws deeply on local talent to discuss a metaphorically rich subject: "how two different experiences can happen at one location." Pinder will reconfigure Birmingham's Lyric Theatre, a vaudeville house turned movie palace, as a site for reenacting cultural battles. When the Lyric closed its doors in 1958, it was the only theater in Birmingham where blacks could watch a performance at the same time as whites, albeit from a segregated balcony.

Revisiting the Jim Crow era and recharging the energy of the space, *Belly of the Beast* will place a black gospel choir in the balcony and a white bluegrass choir in the orchestra pit. "Both of those styles of music are completely about passion and devotion," Pinder says, "and we try to draw together the distinct qualities of each of them and create new sounds. But no way is this going to be a concert." Instead it's an immersive study in harmony and dissonance, with dramatic conflict taking the form of musical sparring. "It's almost like a duel," the artist continues. Influences range from Sacred Harp to the contemporary pop chart: "What would it sound like if a bluegrass group could reinterpret Kanye West?"

Pinder's artistic process led to an unprecedented cross-pollination. "Even within the gospel community, these choirs don't regularly get chances to sing with each other." The beauty of this *Beast*—and of Jefferson Pinder's work in general—lies in its ability to provoke meaningful dialogue.

By Troy Patterson, the writer-at-large for Slate .com, who has written about books, television and the arts for the New York Times Book Review, GQ *and* Entertainment Weekly

THE DREAM TODAY

IN SOME WAYS, AMERICA HAS EXCEEDED KING'S
VISION. IN OTHERS, HOWEVER, HIS TO-DO LIST
REMAINS FAR FROM FINISHED

BY MICHELE NORRIS

I SPENT MUCH of the summer of 2013 talking to people who witnessed Martin Luther King Jr.'s speech 50 years earlier. While reaching back through time to understand that day, I collected a series of photographs of King on my computer. At some point I noticed something in these images. In most of them, King's arm is outstretched toward the crowd, hand held high, palm open, the way you might raise hands over someone in church who is standing in need of prayer. As my reporting took me back to 1963—a year of tumult and bloodshed in the fight for racial equality—I realized that as King was reaching out over the crowd, he might as well have been reaching up to touch the sun.

The things he mused about in that speech were the stuff of fantasy in 1963. You needed more than just the audacity of hope to imagine that states "sweltering with the heat of oppression" could be "transformed into an oasis of freedom and justice." Even things that seem routine today

Looking Ahead
Austin Brown, 9,
of Gainesville, Ga.,
at the March on
Washington in 1963.

were well outside the bounds of reasonable expectations in 1963. So how far have we come since that hot August day? Has King's dream been achieved?

In some ways the America of today has even exceeded what he allowed himself to envision. Fifty years after King delivered his speech, another black man stood at the Lincoln Memorial to address the masses, this time at a lectern embellished with a presidential seal. And the crowd assembled to hear Barack Obama included women, minorities and immigrants who had climbed a ladder of upward mobility that simply did not exist five decades ago. There were also people in that crowd who could look into their own past and remember a time when they once enforced or embraced segregation, not necessarily out of hatred but because that is just the way it was. Rabid segregationists may have been the pistons that kept Jim Crow segregation humming, but apathy and the go-along-to-get-along mentality fueled the engine of racist America.

King knew that, and it is why throughout 1963 his speeches, his interviews and his "Letter from a Birmingham Jail" were aimed not just at dispossessed blacks but also at "do nothingism" among moderate whites who he said were "more devoted to 'order' than to justice." When you look at those two historic tent poles spanning half a century—the preacher and the president—it is clear that irrefutable aspects of King's dream have been realized. King's lawyer Clarence Jones, who helped draft the March on Washington speech, said those who worked closely with King "never contemplated the possibility of a black president in our lifetimes."

But as we measure progress since that day in August, are we using the right mile stick?

America twice elected a president who is black. That's one for the history books—but so too was the day that same president visited the White House briefing room to remind America that while the world rises up to meet him as a leader, as a black man he might have a hard time hailing a cab. Speaking of the not-guilty verdict in the Trayvon Martin case, Obama said, "I think it is important to recognize that the African American community is looking at this issue through a set of experiences and a history that doesn't go away." With that statement, the distance between the preacher and the president was much like an image in an automobile's side-view mirror: objects in mirror are closer than they appear.

It can often seem that King's dream has almost completely upstaged his to-do list. The full name of the 1963 event was the March on Washington for Jobs and Freedom. Planners distributed organizing manuals that detailed the reasons for the grand effort—"What We Demand," the manual stated. The answer was a 10-point plan that included "dignified jobs at decent wages," "desegregation of all school districts" and a ban on discrimination in "all housing supported by federal funds."

"Why We March": the manual spelled that out too. "To redress old grievances and to help resolve an American crisis ... born of the twin evils of racism and economic deprivation." That last bit got lost over the years. How does one assess the current state of King's dream without also examining the items on that wish list that have yet to be realized? There is little doubt that had he lived, King today would be concerned about prison rates, murder rates, wars and persistent racial inequality—the so-called opportunity gap. That specific list of demands for the March on Washington for Jobs and Freedom also suggests that King would be particularly upset about the growing wealth gap.

Consider the cruel irony in a now familiar image. King's name adorns major thoroughfares in many American cities, and most often the name of the civil rights icon is attached to streets that run through communities of color. But those streets are too often boulevards of broken dreams and limited opportunities. While the black and Latino middle class is growing, financial stability still remains beyond reach for a large sector of society. Since the mid-1970s, the unemployment

MEASURING THE DREAM

OVER THE PAST 50 YEARS, AFRICAN AMERICANS HAVE SEEN PROFOUND IMPROVEMENTS IN EDUCATIONAL AND ECONOMIC OPPORTUNITIES, BUT A CLEAR RACIAL GAP REMAINS

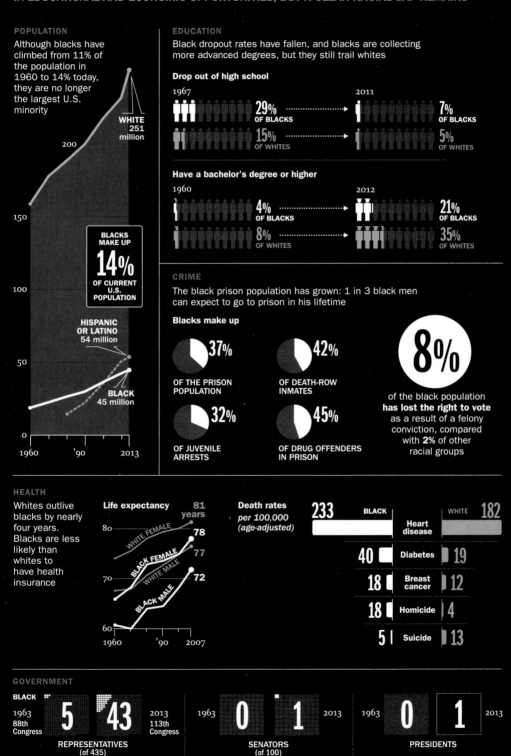

POPULATION

Although blacks have climbed from 11% of the population in 1960 to 14% today, they are no longer the largest U.S. minority

WHITE
251 million

200

150

BLACKS MAKE UP 14% OF CURRENT U.S. POPULATION

100

HISPANIC OR LATINO
54 million

50

BLACK
45 million

0

1960   '90   2013

EDUCATION

Black dropout rates have fallen, and blacks are collecting more advanced degrees, but they still trail whites

Drop out of high school

1967
29% OF BLACKS → 2011 7% OF BLACKS
15% OF WHITES → 5% OF WHITES

Have a bachelor's degree or higher

1960
4% OF BLACKS → 2012 21% OF BLACKS
8% OF WHITES → 35% OF WHITES

CRIME

The black prison population has grown: 1 in 3 black men can expect to go to prison in his lifetime

Blacks make up

37% OF THE PRISON POPULATION

42% OF DEATH-ROW INMATES

32% OF JUVENILE ARRESTS

45% OF DRUG OFFENDERS IN PRISON

8% of the black population **has lost the right to vote** as a result of a felony conviction, compared with **2%** of other racial groups

HEALTH

Whites outlive blacks by nearly four years. Blacks are less likely than whites to have health insurance

Life expectancy

81 years
80
WHITE FEMALE — 78
BLACK FEMALE — 77
WHITE MALE — 72
70
BLACK MALE
60
1960   '90   2007

Death rates *per 100,000 (age-adjusted)*

	BLACK		WHITE
Heart disease	233		182
Diabetes	40		19
Breast cancer	18		12
Homicide	18		4
Suicide	5		13

GOVERNMENT

BLACK

REPRESENTATIVES (of 435)
1963 88th Congress: 5 — 43: 2013 113th Congress

SENATORS (of 100)
1963: 0 — 1: 2013

PRESIDENTS
1963: 0 — 1: 2013

About 25% of black families live below the poverty
line today—down from 41% in the mid-1960s

Poverty rate

10% 20 30 40%+
Blacks in poverty

WASH. ORE. IDAHO MONT. WYO. NEV. UTAH CALIF. ARIZ. N.M. N.D. S.D. NEB. COLO. KANS. OKLA. TEXAS MINN. IOWA MO. ARK. WIS. ILL. IND. KY. TENN. MISS. LA. MICH. OHIO W.VA. VA. N.C. S.C. ALA. GA. PA. N.Y. D.C. MD. DEL. N.J. VT. N.H. MAINE MASS. R.I. CONN. FLA.

ALASKA
HAWAII

Maine
has the highest
black unemployment
rate **(21%)** and the
highest black
poverty rate **(46%)**

New York
has the highest
percentage of black
business owners,
11%

Mississippi
is one of the
poorest states, but
it has the highest
percentage of black
homeowners **(56%)**

Median income
2011 dollars

WHITE
$27,000

$20k

BLACK
$21,000

$10k

0

1960 '70 '80 '90 2000 2011

The median
income for black
men is **67%** that of
white men. The
median income for
black women is **92%**
that of white women

Unemployment rate
Through strong economic
times and recessions,
black unemployment has
hovered at roughly double
white unemployment

2013
WHITE
7%

BLACK
MEN
15%

BLACK
WOMEN
13%

BLACKS
AGE 20–24
23%

BLACKS
AGE 60–64
9%

7% of businesses were owned by blacks
in 2007—**more than triple** the
percentage in 1967

45% of blacks now own their own homes,
compared with **70%** of whites

rate for blacks has consistently been roughly double the jobless rate for whites. Even the concept
of wealth is relative when assessed in black and white terms. The median wealth of black families
in which the head of household graduated from college is less than the median wealth for white
families whose head of household dropped out of high school. Eighty-five percent of black and
Latino households have a net worth that falls below the median wealth for white households.
Closing the gap would require black and Latino households to save 100% of their incomes for
three consecutive years. Talk about trying to touch the sun.

In the decades following the March on Washington, much of the work focused on integration.
It was often about terrain: Who got to go to what schools or live in what neighborhoods? Who
had access to the management track? There were busing, affirmative action, equal-opportunity
programs and diversity training. The result of all those efforts can be summed up quite powerfully in six simple words: "We wanted equality. We got integration."

Those six words recently arrived in my inbox from Rondrea Danielle Mathis of Tampa. For
the past three years I have been collecting six-word stories on race and cultural identity at the
Race Card Project to help foster a dialogue on differences and to better understand the experience of race in America. Tens of thousands of people have shared their stories, and collectively
they provide potent lessons for us all. One of the things I came to realize during this summer
retrospective is that the equality King called for involves not physical terrain but the geography
of the mind. What kind of baggage do we carry? What assumptions do we make? What kinds of
boxes do we put people in—or even create for ourselves?

Try this exercise. Read the following descriptions and visualize the people from these sce-
narios in your mind: A banker. A law-school valedictorian. A family out on a Sunday afternoon
hoping to purchase a new home. A man who spends his retirement fly-fishing. The woman who

■ Are relations between whites and blacks very good, somewhat good, somewhat bad or very bad?

Very or somewhat good

66% **72%**
BLACKS WHITES

■ Are new civil rights laws needed to reduce discrimination against blacks?

Yes

53% **17%**
BLACKS WHITES

■ Do you favor programs that make special efforts to help blacks and other minorities get ahead to make up for past discrimination?

Yes

81% **61%**
BLACKS WHITES

■ Do you approve or disapprove of the way Barack Obama is handling race relations?

Approve

78% **41%**
BLACKS WHITES

■ Do you think the American justice system is biased against black people?

Yes

68% **25%**
BLACKS WHITES

■ Do you support a law for your state that says people can fight back with deadly force if they feel threatened, even if they could retreat?

Support

37% **57%**
BLACKS WHITES

■ Are you satisfied or dissatisfied with the Zimmerman verdict?

Satisfied

5% **49%**
BLACKS WHITES

TIME research by Emily Maltby and Alex Aciman

Note: Income data from 2002 to the present and population data from 2000 to the present include those who identify as two or more races.

Sources: U.S. Census Bureau; *Digest of Education Statistics;* NAACP; Federal Bureau of Prisons; Bureau of Justice Statistics; the Sentencing Project; Bureau of Labor Statistics; University of Washington; National Center for Health Statistics; Congressional Research Service; Gallup; Public Religion Research Institute; Quinnipiac; Pew

is juggling family, work and aging parents and still trying to make a weekly yoga class.

Now be honest. What did the people look like? Did they resemble members of your family or people in your community? Were the images based on what you see and hear in your life or in the media? Did that bank president have a South Asian name that included so many syllables that it seemed to dance across the tongue? Did that law-school valedictorian give a shout-out to grandparents in the audience who have prospered in America but do not speak fluent English?

Most likely the answers are no. But by 2023, the majority of children under 18 in this country will be minorities. And yes, that will call for a new terminology—but also a new way of thinking. The socioeconomic indicators that once marked people for automatic privilege are shifting. The next generation of 18-year-olds isn't going to look or sound like the last. If America is to prosper, kids who listen to reggaeton, eat kimchi, celebrate their quinceañeras, work weekends at the small-town Dairy Queen and wear oversize hoodies have to believe in the promise of King's dream. The geography of the mind requires that we challenge our assumptions and see past differences to place all kinds of people in a category marked "bound for success." While it is regrettable that King's "unfinished" list is still too long, the brilliance of his riff on the dream was that it challenged us to think differently. King could see the future from where he stood. People of all colors flocked to Washington. The U.S. press did not linger on that fact, but the international press was awestruck by the diversity. Decades later, it is still a focal point when people look to our country from overseas. Our diversity is seen as one of the best things America has going for it. Perhaps we should recognize that too.

Norris is a special correspondent for National Public Radio and director of the Race Card Project (theracecardproject.com).

CREDITS

Cover Photo Researchers/Getty Images; **1** Leonard Freed/Magnum Photos; **2-3** Steve Schapiro/Corbis; **4** (from left) Elliot Erwitt/Magnum; Paul Schutzer/Time & Life Pictures/Getty Images; **5** (from left) Bruce Davidson/Magnum; Pete Souza/White House/Getty Images; **8** Paul Schutzer/Time & Life Pictures/Getty Images; **11** (from left) Apic/Getty Images; Mansell/Time & Life Pictures/Getty Images; Stock Montage/Getty Images; **13** (from left) Timepix/Time & Life Pictures/Getty Images; Library of Congress/Time & Life Pictures/Getty Images; Schomburg Center, NYPL/Art Resource, NY; **14-15** Don Cravens/Time & Life Pictures/Getty Images; **16** Francis Miller/Time & Life Pictures/Getty Images; **17** Howard Sochurek/Time & Life Pictures/Getty Images; **18-19** Charles Moore/Black Star; **20-21** Dan Budnik/Contact Press Images; **22-23** Gordon Parks/LIFE; **24-25** Bruce Davidson/Magnum; **26-27** Dan Budnik/Contact Press Images; **29** AP Photo; **31** Robert W. Kelley/Time & Life Pictures/Getty Images; **32** Bob Parent/Getty Images; **35** Fred Ward/Award Agency; **36** Marco Grob for TIME/courtesy National Museum of American History; **37** Marco Grob for TIME; **39-40** Marco Grob for TIME; **43** Marco Grob for TIME; **44-45** Dan Budnik/Contact Press Images; **46-52** Marco Grob for TIME; **54-55** Express Newspapers/Getty Images; **57** Marco Grob for TIME; **58** (clockwise from top left) Marco Grob for TIME/Collection of Walter Naegle (3); Marco Grob for TIME/courtesy National Museum of American History (2); **59** (clockwise from top left) Marco Grob for TIME/courtesy National Museum of American History (2); Marco Grob for TIME/Collection of Joan Baez; Marco Grob for TIME/courtesy National Museum of American History (2); **61** Marco Grob for TIME; **62-63** ©Bob Adelman; **65** ©Flip Schulke; **69** Bettmann/Corbis; **70** Steve Schapiro/Corbis; **73** Gordon Parks/LIFE; **74** AP Photo; **75** Birmingham News/Landov; **77** Vernon Merritt/Birmingham News/Landov; **78** AP Photo/Hal Yeager; **81** Bettmann/Corbis; **83** AP Photo; **84** Frank Dandridge/Time & Life Pictures/Getty Images; **86-87** Grey Villet/Time & Life Pictures/Getty Images; **89** John Olson/Time & Life Pictures/Getty Images; **90** Bob Parent/Hulton Archive/Getty Images; **93** Nick Veasey for TIME; **96** Mark Peterson/Redux (2); **97** Mark Peterson/Redux (2); **101, 103-105** Bill Phelps; **107** AP Photo; **112** Photo Researchers/Getty Images; **Back cover** Express Newspapers/Getty Images

TIME

Managing Editor Nancy Gibbs
Design Director D.W. Pine
Director of Photography Kira Pollack

Called to Be Free

Editors Radhika Jones, Stephen Koepp
Designer Christine Dunleavy
Photo Editors Liz Ronk, Phil Bicker
Writers Jeannine Amber, Michelle Alexander, Patrik Henry Bass, John Cloud, Ben Cosgrove, Elizabeth Dias, Charlayne Hunter-Gault, Lani Guinier, Jon Meacham, Michele Norris, Troy Patterson, Kate Pickert, Michael Scherer, Richard Norton Smith, Cynthia Tucker, Jose Antonio Vargas
Reporters Daniel S. Levy, Lina Lofaro, Damien Scott
Editorial Production David Sloan

Time Home Entertainment

Publisher Jim Childs
Vice President, Brand & Digital Strategy Steven Sandonato
Executive Director, Marketing Services Carol Pittard
Executive Director, Retail & Special Sales Tom Mifsud
Executive Publishing Director Joy Butts
Director, Bookazine Development & Marketing Laura Adam
Finance Director Glenn Buonocore
Associate Publishing Director Megan Pearlman
Associate General Counsel Helen Wan
Assistant Director, Special Sales Ilene Schreider
Brand Manager Bryan Christian
Associate Production Manager Kimberly Marshall
Associate Prepress Manager Alex Voznesenskiy

Editorial Director Stephen Koepp
Senior Editor Roe D'Angelo
Copy Chief Rina Bander
Design Manager Anne-Michelle Gallero
Editorial Operations Gina Scauzillo

Special Thanks Katherine Barnet, Brad Beatson, Jeremy Biloon, Susan Chodakiewicz, Rose Cirrincione, Neil Fine, Jacqueline Fitzgerald, Christine Font, Diane Francis, Jenna Goldberg, Hillary Hirsch, David Kahn, Amy Mangus, Nina Mistry, Dave Rozzelle, Ricardo Santiago, Adriana Tierno, Time Inc. Premedia, TIME Research Center, Vanessa Wu

ISBN 10: 1-61893-117-2
ISBN 13: 978-1-61893-117-7
Library of Congress Control Number: 2013951174

We welcome your comments and suggestions about TIME Books. Please write to us at TIME Books, Attention: Book Editors, P.O. Box 11016, Des Moines, IA 50336-1016. If you would like to order any of our hardcover Collector's Edition books, please call us at 800-327-6388, Monday through Friday, 7 a.m. to 8 p.m., or Saturday, 7 a.m. to 6 p.m., Central Time.

'1963 IS N
BUT A B

MART
IN HIS "I HAVE A '